THE MEDITERRANEAN ZEITGEIST

Re-Orienting the Renaissance

METIN MUSTAFA

Essays Series

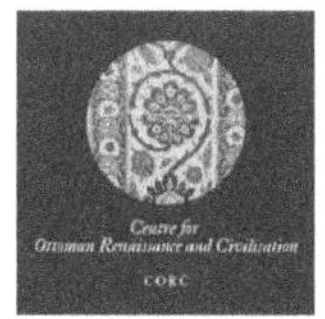

Centre for Ottoman Renaissance and Civilisation
Sydney

Published by Centre for Ottoman Renaissance and Civilisation

Website: ottomanrenaissance.org

Email: info@ottomanrenaissance.org

ISBN: 978-0-646-83544-0

Printed in the United States

Cover design by Centre for Ottoman Renaissance and Civilisation.

Other books by the author:

Renaissance Women:

Nuns, Sultanas and Queens Legitimising Female Sovereignty

Michelangelo meets Sinan:

Representations of the Divine, Salvation and Paradise in Renaissance Art

History of Ottoman Renaissance Art:

From Mehmed I to Selim II. Revised Edition.

The Ottoman Renaissance:

A Reconsideration of Early Modern Ottoman Art, 1413-1575

Tragedy of Sultan Süleyman (a play)

Contents

The Renaissance

❧

The Renaissance is usually associated with the Italian city states like Florence, but Italy's undoubted importance has too often overshadowed the development of new ideas in northern Europe, the Iberian peninsula, the Islamic world, south-east Asia, and Africa. In offering a more global perspective on the nature of the Renaissance, it would be more accurate to refer to a series of 'Renaissances' throughout these regions, each with their own highly specific and separate characteristics. These other Renaissances often overlapped and exchanged influences with the more classical and traditionally understood Renaissance centred on Italy. The Renaissance was a remarkably international, fluid, and mobile phenomenon.

Jerry Brotton, *The Renaissance: A Very Short Introduction* (New York: Oxford University Press, 2006).

❧

Ottoman ideas of rebirth, although built on the classical Greece and Rome, moved well beyond these legacies. Indeed, the Ottomans were much more focused on their Eastern (Turkic, Timurid, Persian) and Islamic heritage than that of the classical world which features in the West. Both the ancient and recent past provided inspiration on which to build a cultural identity specific to the Ottoman artistic experience … The unique geographic location of the sultans of the Ottoman court allowed artists of the Ottoman Empire to capitalise on the inherited legacies of both the Islamic–Timurid–Turkic–Persian East and the Latin West. The result was a synthesis of Eastern and Western exemplars which ultimately produced a rebirth in the arts distinct from their early modern Italian and European counterparts.

Metin Mustafa, *The Ottoman Renaissance: A Reconsideration of Early Modern Ottoman Art, 1413-1575* (New Jersey: Blue Dome Press, 2019).

Understanding "Zeitgeist"

This book is the second part of the essays series that grew out of my doctorate years between 2103 and 2017. My research interests in the idea of many renaissances and cross-cultural interactions in the early modern Mediterranean world between the Ottomans and Europeans provided me with ample scope to delve into multiple aspects of Renaissance cultures of the sixteenth century. The content is of historical significance because it draws on comparative analysis of the accomplishments of early modern Europe and the Ottoman Empire respectively. By re-Orienting the Renaissance, the history of the early modern Mediterranean civilisations in the sixteenth century underscores the shared cultural and artistic heritage.

To make sense of the concept of the Mediterranean *zeitgeist,* particularly during the sixteenth century, it is pertinent to look at the meaning of the word from a sociological perspective. Providing a brief analysis on the concept may provide conceptual insights to frame the basis of the argument the essays in this book elucidate. According to Monkia Krause in the article, 'What is Zeitgeist? Examining period-specific cultural patterns':

> [...] we understand zeitgeist as a hypothesis for a pattern in meaningful practices that is specific to a particular historical time-period, links different realms of social life and social groups, and extends across geographical contexts. As such, the concept of zeitgeist sensitises us to a set of phenomena, which can be described independently of and alongside other cultural phenomena such as trans-historical schemas, binaries, or group-specific patterns.[1]

The meaningful cultural practices experienced in the Mediterranean basin during the sixteenth century provide historians ample examples to compare and contrast the cultural achievements of Europe and the Ottoman Empire respectively. While Karl Mannheim focused on the *zeitgeists* of social groups in *Essays on the Sociology of Knoweldge,* a broader range of cultural phenomena including visual representations of power and identity are excluded.[2] The visual vocabulary of early modern cities are testament to the self-fashioning of early modern rulers in Europe and the Ottoman Empire. Such practices including religious rituals extend beyond confined geographies allowing the idea of *zeitgeist* to "sensitise" us to common cultural experiences specific to a particular historical time-period. It is, therefore, the aim of the essays in this book to provide a discussion that firstly redefines what we mean by the term "Renaissance" in Essay I and then reconsider the patterns of cultural practices in Italy and the Ottoman Empire in the sixteenth century from a revisionist paradigm in Essays II and III respectively.

The three essays in this book explore the distinctive historical location of the Mediterranean basin – Italy and Ottoman Istanbul – respectively, that relate to strong notions of cross-cultural entities. The integrated cultural wholes represented specifically by sixteenth century Venice and Istanbul challenge our understanding of the Vasarian notion of the "Renaissance" and promote a more culturally and globally inclusive definition of the term. According to Warwick Ball:

> After all, where would Galileo be without Ulugh Beg? Vasco da Gama without Ibn Majid? The Italian Renaissance without Umayyad Cordoba? The Greek Classics without Baghdad translation school? Western medicine without Avicenna? ... The point is, there is neither a 'them' nor an 'us': we are all the products of both ... that the definition of 'Europe' be constitutionally enshrined as non-Muslim, or at least non-Turkish – and by extension a Christian union. This not only ignores that two of the great periods of European civilisation – Constantinople in the age of Sultan Süleyman the Magnificent and the Andalusia in the age of Caliph Abd ar-Rahman III – were Muslim ...[3]

The accomplishments of the civilisation of early modern Europe is inconceivable without the achievements of medieval Islam and the Ottoman Empire. It is most pertinent that historians explore the notion of cultural enlightenment in the early modern period from an inclusive paradigm – one that unites rather than erect barriers across civilisations. Exploring the notion of the Mediterranean *zeitgeist* from a culturally inclusive perspective widens our scope of understanding of the "meaningful practices that is specific to a particular historical time-period."[4] These meaningful practices, including architectural accomplishments, hybrid objects of cultural materialism, and the iconography of public ceremonials by the ruling elite, most often include recurring symbolic structures that underpin the idea of the Mediterranean *zeitgeist*. These recurring symbolisms in early modern Europe and the Ottoman Empire respectively underscore the human, cultural and intellectual phenomena that ultimately associate with cultural identity and affirmation of court ceremonial grandeur. It can be argued that the idea of Mediterranean *zeitgeist*, instead of concentrating and elaborating upon the differences between cultural accomplishments, rather celebrate each age or epoch through the central thesis of historicism. According to Mannheim:

> [...] no product of human culture could be analysed and understood in a 'timeless' fashion; interpretation had to begin by ascribing to each product a temporal index, by relating it to a period-bound 'style'... Once the historian had put himself into the antiquarian mood in which he looked at cultural products, not with his own eyes but with the eyes of the denizens of bygone cultures, he was perfectly able to sense a greatness, a human significance, which pervaded the whole historic process throughout its changing and perishable manifestations.[5]

Patterns on meanings are sometimes conjectured with cultures that are constant throughout historical periods. Other times, it can be argued that certain patterns of meanings are at least relatively enduring. By relating a certain historical period to a "style" that is understood in art history, then the aesthetics or the visual vocabulary associated with a historical period is independent of historical location.[6] With this in mind, art created in any given time, by its very nature, is reflective of that particular period. The Hegelian understanding of *zeitgeist* acknowledges that culture and art are inextricable as artists are products of their time, therefore, introducing that culture to any given work of art.[7] In this way, the concept of *zeitgeist* locates cultural achievements via cross-cultural hybridity that promotes cultural inclusiveness rather than focus on differences.

The three essays examine the connection between the idea of *zeitgeist* and an emphatic understanding of the sixteenth century Mediterranean as unified cultural wholes. Through the shared experience of significant historical events in the sixteenth century Mediterranean, we can see cultural currents at play that too often overlap in complex ways. In the first essay, 'The Renaissance Paradigm" A Revisionist Perspective', I challenge the pan-European notions of the "Renaissance". Appreciating the Ottoman attitude to rebirth is integral to understanding the early modern Mediterranean experience and assists a more global perspective of the Renaissance period. Like their Renaissance counterparts in Florence, Venice and other regions in early modern Italy and Europe at the time, the Ottomans too looked to past exemplars to forge a powerful global identity. They too experienced a rebirth, but with a difference. The Ottomans not only propagated the classical heritage of the West, which they inherited at the conquest of Constantinople in 1453, but also exploited the powerful and enduring legacy they shared with their Islamic, Turkic, Perso-Timurid cousins. In this strategic appropriation of both Eastern and Western legacies, the work argues that the Ottomans fashioned a distinctive Renaissance. It is in interrogating the product of this synthesis that the essay makes its original contribution to global Renaissance studies. This essay expressly tests the question: did the Ottomans have a Renaissance? By giving voice to contemporary Renaissance writers and artists including Giorgio Vasari (1511-1574), Mustafa Ali (1541-1600) and Mimar Sinan (1489-1588), the first essay demonstrates the emergence of the the notion of multiple renaissances with distinctive features in the early modern Mediterranean basin.

The second essay, 'The Mediterranean Renaissance: A Shared Heritage', focuses on the European-Islamic / East-West shared cultural legacies of the early modern Europeans and the Ottomans respectively. By the 15th and 16th centuries, with the expansion of the Ottoman Empire under Sultan Mehmed II and Süleyman the Magnificent, the Ottomans experienced a unique period when their art, and Italian art, were experiencing artistic efflorescence. While much scholarly work has been conducted on the political, military, social and cultural history of the Ottoman Empire, there has been little research into how the Renaissance narrative applies to Ottoman visual arts and architecture between Ottoman Istanbul and Renaissance Italy during the period in discussion. This is not due to neglect or oversight, but is rather a conscious decision to avoid 'sameness' with the 'other'. This essay aims to explore the dynamism of Renaissance cultural interconnectedness where cultures worked both independently and collaboratively to create beautiful and inspirational works exemplified by the Mediterranean Renaissance *zeitgeist,* or spirit of the age.

Finally, the third essay in this series, 'The Iconography of Renaissance Ceremonials in the Early Modern World', explores the iconography of Renaissance court ceremonials in the 16th century – how the East influenced the West – before the Orientalist trend and its impact on European visual culture during the latter part of the 17th and 18th centuries. From similar practices of using ceremonials and pageantries as representations of power and dynastic propaganda, to forging imperial and dynastic identities through myths, the Ottoman sultans and the dukes and princes of Florence and the Republic of Venice contributed to cross-cultural connections during the Renaissance period. As a result of this inextricable cultural connection between the Ottoman Empire and Renaissance Italy, this essay argues the view that the Ottomans deserve a place in the Renaissance discourse. In this way, the overarching argument in the essay further emphasises the shared cultural heritage of early modern Europeans and Ottomans with not only classical Greece and Rome, but also of the medieval Islamic civilisation. Therefore, to insist on an exclusively Florentine, Italian, or European *rinascita* or cultural rebirth would fail to appreciate the cultural interconnectedness of the early modern period. In contrast, by recognising Ottoman art as part of a larger Renaissance narrative, the three essays celebrate the shared cultural achievements in the Mediterranean basin during the sixteenth century that epitomised the spirit of the age – the Mediterranean *Zeitgeist*.

The Renaissance Paradigm: A Revisionist Perspective

ESSAY I

INTRODUCTION

The challenge for art historians begins with the term 'Renaissance' and its ever-changing interpretation through the centuries to suit the historical context of the time. The aim of this study is to briefly explore the dominant Vasarian understanding of the Renaissance and its historiographical, indeed historical, impact from the sixteenth to the twenty-first century. By the nineteenth century, the Vasarian context was lost on the new interpreters of Renaissance. Men like Jacob Burckhardt and Jules Michelet took from Vasari's work certain absolute truths of the idea that the Renaissance witnessed the birth of the modern individual. As authoritative scholars in their own right, Jacob Burckhardt (1818-1897) and Jules Michelet (1798-1874) influenced generations, with the Renaissance coming to symbolise the beginning of European modernity. Such modernist perspectives on the Renaissance are now interpreted in the context of nineteenth-century nationalism and colonialism as offering models of civilisation with concomitant ideas of cultural superiority and the right to rule and define the 'Other' through their eyes. The periods of exploration, empire building and European colonisation contributed to the spread of these European ideals. With twentieth-century wars and associated decolonisation, the bubble of civilisation burst and the narrative of Giorgio Vasari's (1511-1574) Renaissance was called into question. Indeed, with the hindsight of the twenty-first century, reframing the definition of Renaissance is a high priority not only for Western scholars but also for non-European scholars, especially for cultures in the Mediterranean basin, which share a historical legacy with their European counterparts.

Directly engaging with this new historiographical trend, the study reshapes the notion of the Renaissance by uniquely looking at Ottoman, rather than Vasarian, understandings of rebirth, specifically through the contemporary works of Mustafa Ali (1541-1600) and Mimar Sinan (1489-1588). This essay, therefore, establishes a more meaningful and specifically Ottoman definition that permits a reading of Ottoman artistic production both within its own context and within a more global one. Beginning with the Vasarian perception of the Renaissance, followed by nineteenth to twenty-first century developments in Renaissance historiography, then continuing with the Ottoman view of the same, the chapter not only reviews the main body of literature in the field but sets up the theoretical foundation for the research as a whole.

With the hindsight of the twenty-first century, reframing the definition of Renaissance is a high priority not only for Western scholars but also for non-European scholars, especially for cultures in the Mediterranean basin, which share a historical legacy with their European counterparts. Directly engaging with a revisionist approach, this study reshapes the notion of the Renaissance by uniquely looking at Ottoman, rather than Vasarian, understandings of rebirth, specifically through the contemporary works of Mustafa Ali and Mimar Sinan.[1] Before exploring the problematic nature of Renaissance historiography, it is crucial to first understand and contextualise the concepts that comprise Vasari's definition of the Renaissance of the arts.

❧

The Vasarian Paradigm

The Renaissance is traditionally associated with the revival of classical Greek and Roman literature, philosophy and art and the aesthetic and intellectual innovations they inspired. In addition, the Renaissance is typically associated with the Florentines of the late fourteenth to mid-sixteenth centuries. Giorgio Vasari's *The Lives of the Painters, Sculptors and Architects* published in 1550 and again in 1565 was its most authoritative written articulation.[2] The Vasarian *rinascita* saw the ideals of progress and perfection as its key qualities.[3] Indeed, within his Tuscan-centric vision, Vasari argued that 'perfection' was attained by Tuscan artists alone. These artists occupied a privileged position in history, appointed by God to revive and indeed surpass the great arts of the ancients and to launch their contemporaries into a bright future entirely embedded in a Christian framework. Vasari's narrative exerted influence well into the twentieth century, being the most influential Renaissance text ever composed in the West.

In its literal translation, the verb *rinascere* means 'to be born again'. In his *Lives,* Vasari uses the term specifically to characterise the stages of art development up until his own day. For Vasari, the perfection of the classical arts in his own time took centuries to attain suggesting that it was an evolving process:

> [...] the rise of the arts to perfection [the classical past], their decline [the Middle Ages] and their restoration or, to say it better, renaissance.[4]

Vasari unambiguously introduces the notion of *rinascita* into the discourse of the time. For Vasari, this rebirth of the arts was a gradual process that took approximately three centuries, beginning with the works of Cimabue (1240–1302) and '...improving little by little from a humble beginning, and finally ... arriv[ing] at the height of perfection'[5] with Michelangelo (1483–1520) in Vasari's own time. This slow trajectory towards perfection evolved through distinctive stages, including *imitazione* (imitation) and *adeguazione* (adaptation), both of which were necessary to surpass the classical models and achieve *perfezione* (perfection) in Vasari's temporal present.

Vasari's narrative is imbued with a humanist impulse typical of his day, with the close imitation of the classical past and the astute adaptation of those models for the present. Emulating the great ancient classical masters like Aristotle and Pliny, the *Lives* is a biographical celebration that links Vasari's context to both past and future, yet maintains a focused relevance to his contemporary day. Such imitation of the past was part and parcel of Vasari's characterisation of the Medici rulers to whom he had dedicated his work. In part three of the text he praised their contributions to the city of Florence in a true Aristotelian manner, signifying the permanence of their magnificence:

> [...] men of rare and beautiful genius, from whom the world receives such beauty, honour, convenience and benefit, deserve to live forever in the minds and memories of mankind.[6]

The panegyric, delivered to promote the excellence of Florence through congratulatory rhetoric and self-aggrandisement, has at its core a desire to claim uncontested superiority. Leonardo Bruni's *Panegyric to the City of Florence* (c. 1401) is a fine precedent for Vasari's civic self-fashioning. In humanistic style, Bruni wrote in imitation of Aelius Aristides' *Panathenicus* (*Panegyric to Athens*, 117–181 CE). Hans Baron argues that Bruni cast his work on the classical model because it spoke directly to contemporary Florentines in the fashioning of their cultural identity. Indeed, Bruni ascribes to Florentines all the virtues associated with Aristides' Athens, well-known even in Vasari's day as the cultural capital of the Greek world, in an attempt to identify Florence as the new Athens of its time.[7]

The path of emulation and imitation was already well-trodden by Vasari's time. From as early as the eleventh century onwards, Vasari informs us that artists began adapting and imitating classical remnants. In the Duomo of Santa Maria Assunta in Siena in 1016 the Pisan architect Buschetto relied on:

> [...] endless quantity of spoils brought by sea from various distant parts, as the columns, bases, capitals, cornices and other stones ... of all sizes, great, medium, and small ... Buschetto displayed great judgment and skill in adapting them to their places ... the façade ... consisting of a great number of columns, adorning it with other carved columns and antique statues.[8]

The adaptation of classical remains went hand in hand with the imitation of past precedents. By the fourteenth century Tuscan architects were imitating classical doors, windows, columns, arches and cornices '... carved by the hand of Andrea Taffi with the same Greek manner, but indeed much more beautiful in the church of San Giovanni in their city'.[9] In the Church of Santa Maria della Spina in Pisa (1323), Giovanni Pisano's works of sculpture 'brought ornaments in that oratory to that perfection that is seen today'.[10] For Vasari, Pisano demonstrated 'grace', 'style', and 'excellence' of invention, which he saw as prerequisites for distinction.[11]

In order to surpass the greats of the antique past, the Renaissance artists' challenge required skill. For Vasari, this meant the artist had to demonstrate precision, intellect and patience. According to Vasari, Michelangelo was one such man, who 'gave his attention only to the perfection of art' to attain a higher 'degree of refinement' and this could be only realised through devotion to 'minute' and 'delicate' details.[12]

Michelangelo's *David* (1501–1504) clothed in God's glory epitomises His perfection and the Christian message of man's triumph. This first revival of the ancient male nude in monumental form standing over four metres tall depicts its subject patiently waiting for battle against the giant Goliath. As a Christian hero writ large, *David* overshadowed any extant antique sculpture of comparable character. This Renaissance representation of the figure is appropriated from the ancient Greek standing heroic male nude *The Doryphorus* (450–400 BCE), which is thought of as a distinctive style of antique sculpture. The nudes of Greco-Roman art are conceptually perfected ideal persons of heroic qualities, and *David* epitomised the *rebirth* of the 'perfect' Renaissance Christian hero.

Both the *Doryphorus* and *David* statues are in the same *contrapposto* pose. The right leg carries the weight with the left leg slightly behind suggesting movement. Both have their weapon of choice on their left arm. Although the spear is no longer there, it too would have rested on Doryphorus's left shoulder. Like *Doryphorus,* the sculpture of *David* effectively conveys to the viewer the feeling that David is in motion, an impression heightened by his *contrapposto* stance, the twist in his body heightening the figure's animation. In the Biblical context of Michelangelo's *David* ready to face battle against Goliath, David appears to take a moment between conscious choice and action—a man of logical thinking and reason—a Renaissance trait that characterised humanist thought of the time.[13] His facial expression looks drawn, his neck tense and the bulging veins on his right hand reflect this. Like his classical hero counterparts, *David* stands ready to face his giant enemy, about to demonstrate heroic qualities, clothed and protected by God in his 'perfect' form because it is only through this perfection that he can truly defeat his adversary.

Michelangelo achieves this impression of perfection by foreshortening of the body and sacrificing perfect proportions to accommodate the viewers' intended position below the sculpture, enlarging the hands and eyes for narrative effect. In this way, by adjusting the 'perfect' Greek model for dramatic effect, Michelangelo's *David* becomes a Christian hero, for which he ultimately is more perfect than the statues of pagans celebrated since antiquity. With *David,* Michelangelo's work reflected the rebirth of the classical beauty of the human body as well as the Christian God's handiwork. In Vasari's words, Michelangelo's *David* surpassed the ancient nude:

> [...] [w]hen it was built up, and all was finished, he uncovered it, and it cannot be denied that this work has carried off the palm from all other statues, modern or ancient, Greek or Latin.[14]

According to Vasari, Michelangelo's genius made him unparalleled:

> [...] no one ... has ever equalled him in perfection of finish [and] that, wherever he turned his thought, brain, and mind, he displayed such divine power in his works, that, in giving them their perfection, no one was ever his peer in readiness, vivacity, excellence, beauty, and grace. [15]

For Vasari, the perfection in art attained by Michelangelo solidified his triumph over the past. This surpassing of the past further echoed Vasari's Florentine panegyric of Tuscan cultural achievements. Vasari's classical paralleling is explicit. Indeed, he modelled his art history on the elder Pliny's *Natural History* (77–79 CE), but of course Florence and its artists, in Vasari's humanist adaptation, were considered a superior version of the ancient world, because of their Christian underpinning.

Vasari's rebirth narrative took place within a Christian framework, thus offering a contextually convincing argument for Florence's singular superiority in the arts. As part of his Christian worldview, Vasari understood the Tuscan achievement in cosmological and eschatological terms, with Florence (and Florentine artists) at the centre of the earth and indeed central to God's greater salvific plan. It was through their deeds and skill that the mysteries of the divine plan were revealed to humanity. In a neo-Platonic way, they stood as imperfect signposts of the perfection of God. According to the Vasarian narrative, perfection in art in the sixteenth century was only possible through a Christian 'spark' where the truth of the Creator's greater cosmos—its perfection, longevity and existence beyond time—was being slowly revealed to man through engagement in creation. Such a privilege was exclusive to Christians and thus even the great artists of Greece and Rome would always be subordinate, never attaining Vasarian perfection. As Vasari states in the *Lives*:

> Thus the first model from which the first image of man arose was a clod of earth, and not without reason, for the Divine Architect of time and of nature, being all perfection, wished to demonstrate, in the imperfection of His materials, what could be done to improve them, just as good sculptors and painters are in the habit of doing, when, by adding additional touches and removing blemishes, they bring their imperfect sketches to such a state of completion and of perfection as they desire.[16]

This Platonic concept of the Prime Mover as craftsman or *artifex maximus* recalls the Christian evocations of God as Deus Faber, the divine craftsman and creator of the world.

Thus, the Vasarian notion of historical consciousness interprets these ontological phenomena of the starting point of the world as, according to Ulrich Libbrecht, a 'real but imperfect becoming'.[17] From the humanist perspective, the man-artist is a shadow of the perfect Deus Faber. Thus, all man-made precedents imitating nature represent the imperfections of reality. These imperfections are in constant need of refinement or revision. The humanist project of 'imitating' and 'restoring' the great but imperfect ancient art forms was essential to attaining a state of near 'perfection' which, in Vasari's view, was most diligently expressed in the art of his own time and city. For Vasari:

> [O]ur art consists entirely of imitation, first of Nature, and then, as it cannot rise so high of itself, of those things which are produced from the masters with the greatest reputation.[18]

Because of their Christian belief and God's alleged partiality for them, the Florentine artists in particular saw their role as the privileged recipients of God's cosmic message and it is they who constantly strove through the process of imitation to reach perfection. The Vasarian *rinascita* paradigm thus essentially became self-aggrandising in its aim, glorifying Florence as the pinnacle of God's creation as witnessed through the 'perfection [of] the art … among the Tuscans'.[19]

This construct of progress in the arts allowed Vasari to construct a powerful cultural discourse. In keeping with Rüsen's idea of historical understanding, to make sense of the rebirth of the classical arts in his own time, Vasari needed to connect the past convincingly with the present.[20] Vasari's narrative relies on contemporary historical consciousness to make the claim to the cultural triumph of his time; that is, to identify Florence as the pinnacle of artistic evolution.

Vasari's definition of *rinascita,* therefore, is multi-dimensional. First, he argues that the rebirth of art was a slow evolutionary progression clearly discernible in the greater arts of painting, sculpture and architecture. The perfection it professes entailed engaging in a number of developmental stages, entailing *imitazione* and *adeguazione* of the past in order to reach a state of perfection in the sixteenth century. Surpassing the past, the final stage of *rinascita,* was tied inexorably to God's cosmic plan for the world which He, in Vasari's view, invested in the wholly Christianised Republic of Florence.

Historiography: The nineteenth century, nationalism and colonialism

From the Vasarian perspective the perceived superiority of painting, sculpture, and architecture and the consequent inferior status of the fine arts impacted Western perceptions of all so-called minor arts in the West like tapestries, ceramics, and gold smithing. This also had an impact on Islamic artistic expression. As Denny states that:

> … once understood, it not only opens up new horizons of artistic accomplishment to our eyes, but in effect liberates us from the straitjacket of the European 'fine arts' mentality that for five

> centuries has decreed the primacy of painting, sculpture, and architecture, and the inferior status of everything else.[21]

As part of that discourse, painting, sculpture and architecture continued to reign supreme. This perception of inferior status of the fine arts may explain one of the reasons for the lack of receptivity of Ottoman art in the West.

By the seventeenth century, perceptions of the 'Other' in the orientalist discourse led Gottfried Wilhelm Leibniz (1646–1716) to acknowledge the lack of receptivity of the Ottoman civilisation. He described Ottoman lands as places:

> [where the a]rts are not honoured; the inhabitants make no effort to improve cultivation of the land, nor do they attempt to build structures that might endure.[22]

In the nineteenth century Leroy-Bealieu, a stanch supporter of European imperialist ambitions, boasts about European greatness having attained civilisational maturity and strength through its colonial ventures. For Leroy-Bealieu such global significance is limited to only 'civilised people'.[23] These political and cultural views resonated within the Renaissance paradigm defined by Vasari in the sixteenth century, exemplifying European achievements. Continuing to reinvent and adapt itself to different times, the *rinascita* of Vasari thus took on a more nationalistic fervour with the emergence of modern European consciousness. The anachronistic application of the Vasarian 'rebirth' paradigm in the nineteenth century made the Renaissance an exclusive pan-European phenomenon. When Jules Michelet and Jacob Burckhardt applied the term 'Renaissance' only to French and Italian experience respectively they were writing history from a perspective that took Europe's position of global dominance as an ultimate truth. Both men saw France and Italy as the quintessential spiritual and creative triumph of European history and the

Vasarian paradigm thus became easily malleable to their worldview.[24]

Nineteenth century egalitarian principles of the French Revolution were deeply rooted in his understanding of the term 'Renaissance'. For Michelet, the 'Renaissance' meant:

> [...] the discovery of the world and the discovery of man. The sixteenth century ... went from Columbus to Copernicus, from Copernicus to Galileo, from the discovery of the earth to that of the heavens. Man refound himself.[25]

According to Michelet, the Renaissance represented nineteenth century values like Reason, Truth, Art, and Beauty. Michelet became the first modern thinker to define the Renaissance as a decisive historical period in which a crucial break with the Middle Ages took place in European culture. But, for Michelet, the Renaissance happened in France in the sixteenth century and not in the fourteenth and fifteenth centuries Italy. Brotton claims that:

> [a]s a French nationalist, Michelet was eager to claim the Renaissance as a French phenomenon. As a republican, he also rejected what he saw as fourteenth century Italy's admiration for church and political tyranny as deeply undemocratic, and hence excluded these from the spirit of the Renaissance.[26]

For Michelet, the French Revolution was a key moment in history where the birth of the secular French nation brought the country from the darkness of medievalism to enlightenment.

While Michelet saw France as the centre of European Renaissance, the Swiss historian Jacob Burckhardt defined it as a fifteenth-century Italian phenomenon. In 1860 Burckhardt published his view on history with *The Civilisation of the Renaissance in Italy.* Burckhardt saw the Italian Renaissance as a culture in transition. For him, the Renaissance was the birthplace of modern Europe. He described the Italian Renaissance as 'the mother of our own [age] ... whose influence is still at work'.[27] The role of the individual in Renaissance society was important for Burckhardt, who was writing at the time of the unification of Italy, which was becoming a nation for the first time thus influencing him to form a nationalist framework for the Renaissance.

With the birth of Eurocentric interpretation of the Renaissance in the nineteenth century, Burckhardt, like Vasari, made no room for 'the Other'. The Renaissance was defined as an exclusively European phenomenon. It was Italy that gave birth to 'Renaissance Man', who was what Burckhardt called 'the firstborn among the sons of modern Europe'.[28] For later historians, Wallace K. Ferguson and Martin L. McLaughlin, however, the view of the Renaissance as having ushered in the era of modernity occurred much later:

> Confined at first to a rebirth of art or of classical culture, the notion of the Renaissance was broadened as scholars of each successive generation added to it what they regarded as the essence of modern, as opposed to medieval civilization. [29]

Nineteenth-century scholars and thinkers located 'evidence' of the modern in the Renaissance past, tracing the great aspects convincingly to their own day. Their desire to cast the achievements of Renaissance civilisation within a nationalist framework as the epitome of human accomplishments (that is, their accomplishments) has caused problems in art historical discourse and neglected the shared cultural values in the Mediterranean basin.[30]

Orientalism and 'the Other'

If nineteenth century Renaissance discourses encouraged a general disregard of non-European cultural achievements, Orientalism proved even more problematic. The Orient was a framework created by Europeans, which enabled them to view themselves as superior to the Eastern 'Other'. With the publication of Edward Said's *Orientalism* in 1978 the term has become more prevalent in academic discourse of cultural theorists. According to Said:

> [I]ndeed it can be argued that the major component in European culture is precisely what made that culture hegemonic both in and outside Europe: the idea of European identity as a superior one in comparison with all the non-European peoples and cultures ... In a quite constant way, Orientalism depends for its strategy on this flexible positional superiority, which puts the Westerner in a whole series of possible relationships with the Orient without ever losing him the relative upper hand.[31]

The imposition of cultural imperialism enforced upon the societies of the Near East reinforces Said's idea of the cultural hegemony that politically justifies Western imperialism and domination. Cultural imperialism represents non-European societies as culturally static and underdeveloped, thereby forcing them to be dependent on the Europeans to become 'civilised' and 'educated.' The fabrication of this cultural superiority means that the 'Other' can be studied, depicted, and reproduced from a European perspective. Indeed, art historian Erwin Panofsky criticised historians for not showing 'professional interest in the aesthetic aspects of civilisation' – i.e. all civilisations.[32] This rebuke underscores the academic neglect of the achievements of the 'Other'. According to Brotton:

> Renaissance Europe defined and measured itself in relation to the wealth and splendour of the east, a fact that has been overlooked due to the influence of the nineteenth-century version of the Renaissance until recently.[33]

The cultural imperialism of Orientalist narratives allowed the creation of the 'civilisational Other' to justify and legitimise global domination through European colonialism. In the name of modernity, progress, and cultural superiority, cultural imperialism has contributed to the alienation and marginalisation of non-European cultural achievements.

The growing orientalist literature produced by travellers to the Ottoman Empire and the Orient from the sixteenth century onwards also contributed to the marginilisation of the Ottoman 'Other' and stunted the West's reception of Ottoman art. However, according to Edward Said, any European interest in Islam and the Ottomans was not the result of natural curiosity but rather was based in fear about the 'threats' posed by the Muslim 'Other'.[34] Paradoxically, some Europeans actually admired the military power of the Ottomans, but this had little impact on the historiography. Some visitors to the Ottoman Empire published accounts of their voyages, and descriptions of the lands of the 'Other' in writing, illustrations and paintings. According to Ziauddin Sardar their tales 'about Orientalism' contained nothing that was 'neutral or objective'. Sardar believes that '[b]y definition it is a partial and partisan subject'.[35] For Sardar the Orient that was closest to Europe attained the character that ultimately marked all the other Orients.[36] Without the Ottoman Turks there would not have been orientalism, just as the Crusades would have been unthinkable without Islam in the Middle Ages. Similarly, Claire Norton asserts:

> As such the Ottoman Empire is figured as a quintessential Islamic, oriental, or Asian empire, where such terms carry the frequently pejorative connotations common in orientalist discourse ... Very little attention has therefore been given to the extent to which the Ottoman Empire benefited from, participated in and contributed to [via its cultural tradition], what, has been categorised and defined as the Renaissance.[37]

The ambivalent perceptions of the Orientalist therefore perpetuated an indifferent approach to Ottomans' own contributions to the Renaissance discourse. This critical distance between East and West, between the *civilised* and *non-civilised,* is further explored by postcolonial discourse. Like that of Said's *Orientalism,* postcolonial explanations problematise the Renaissance, arguing that foreign cultures can never be presented objectively because of the mediation impacts of language, power and appropriation.[38] According to Stuart Hill:

> [...] power produces new discourses, new kinds of knowledge (i.e. Orientalism), new objects of knowledge (the Orient), it shapes new practices (colonization) and institutions (colonial government).[39]

In the context of representation, Hill argues that 'the circularity of power becomes 'especially important' because 'everyone—the powerful and the powerless—is caught up'.[40] By representing the 'Other' through its eyes, the cultural supremacy of an emerging modern Europe dismissed the achievements of its cultural and ideological adversary.

Representing the 'Other' justifies the dominance of the one who is doing the representing. Therefore, the pan-European Renaissance movement, combined with the narrative of Orientalism, cemented the nineteenth-century paradigm of writers like Michelet and Burckhardt. This paradigm declared France and Italy respectively as the quintessential spiritual and creative triumph of European history. In the orientalist narratives of Michelet and Burckhardt, the Ottoman Empire had no place and was merely perceived as a menace—an alien society. Gerald MacClean sums up the challenging and problematic nature of the nineteenth century construct of the Renaissance as follows:

> If the nineteenth century needed to historicise the artistic achievements of fourteenth- and fifteenth-century Italy by declaring them to signal a rebirth of European magnificence and civilisation, it also needed to ignore the great civilising achievements of the

> Ottomans by viewing that empire as it were a latter-day version of Rome, doomed to decay and fall.[41]

This review of the impact of Renaissance and Orientalist historiography demonstrates the need for this re-examination of early modern Ottoman art. Although sharing some similar traits with their other Renaissance counterparts, namely with Italy, with the emphasis on the East rather than the classical West, this study argues that the Ottomans forged their distinct and separate cultural rebirth in the early modern period. In this way, I argue for an Ottoman rebirth that was different from other contemporaneous renaissances in the Mediterranean, not inferior. Removing the nineteenth-century Eurocentric Renaissance gloss and integrating Vasari's ideas of art as cultural *progress* into a more culturally inclusive narrative allows the exploration of different instances of rebirth with specific and separate characteristics, as expressed by Burioni and Brotton above. In this way, my inclusion of the 'great civilising achievements' of the 'Other' in the Renaissance narrative will both support Necipoğlu's call for 'a fresh narrative' and invite art historians to consider the Renaissance accomplishments of the Ottomans.

Modern revisionist historiography

From the late 1990s revisionist historians began pointing out the problematic nature of orientalism and called for a more inclusive approach to the early modern period. In *Global Interest: Renaissance Art Between East and West*, Lisa Jardine and Jerry Brotton challenge Edward Said's problematic theory of orientalism by negating Said's dominant binary construction of 'us' and 'them'. Jardine and Brotton argue that:

> [...] such arguments enable us to circumvent an account of the marginalized, exoticized, dangerous East within the Renaissance studies as not only politically unhelpful but also historically inaccurate.[42]

Where Said's *Orientalism* problematised the relationship between East and West, Jardine and Brotton moved toward dissolving boundaries and instead argued for the existence of a more receptive interactive experience between East and West.[43] They suggested that once this oppositional orientalist narrative was dismantled, it would negate the belief in 'the antithetical, dark, dirty, exotic, Eastern Other as the negative to which that humane individualism has been opposed—the other ostensibly held at bay by its constructed version of civilization.'[44] This is how modern historiography is addressing the Renaissance and is an approach, which directly underpins this study.

Lisa Jardine also explores this notion of a broader, shared Renaissance in another work, *Worldly Goods: A New History of the Renaissance*. She looks at the material culture of 'the Age' when Renaissance culture in Italy stretched from its western borders in Christendom to the eastern reaches of the Islamic Ottoman Empire, 'bringing this opulent epoch to life in all its material splendor and competitive acquisitiveness'.[45]

The contribution of such revisionist discourse to re-evaluating east-west interaction in the period remains invaluable, however it only focuses on the influence of the East's material culture on the West. It sees the East's contributions to the Renaissance as merely stimulating the creation, production and promulgation of such objects of cultural exchange. Deborah Howard's efforts to illustrate how Islamic elements have been appropriated into Venetian narratives stresses the impact that the former had on the latter but fails to explore the reverse argument. Instead, she addresses broader issues that arose from the material exchanges that contributed hybrid works and shared cultural inheritances in the early modern period of the Mediterranean.

Such reconciliatory efforts to dissolve boundaries can only improve the art history debate and move the discourse toward a more objective analysis of the art of the 'Other'. Yet this can only be achieved by recognising these material objects as products of vibrant and dynamic societies that had themselves undergone a period of transformation, revival and renewal. According to Deborah Howard, '[t]he concept of East and West remains fundamental to our political, ideological and cultural framework.' [46] Culturally-inclusive approaches to the revisionist debate underscore the continual interest in the notion of Renaissance and the ongoing research needed to recognise the many 'Renaissances throughout the regions, each with their own highly specific and separate characteristics' and to acknowledge 'a wider variety of instances of rebirth'.[47]

Recent work by Rosamond Mack, *Bazaar to Piazza: Islamic Trade and Italian Art, 1300–1600*, is part of a growing body of scholarly work that focuses on the artistic exchanges that occurred during the Renaissance in the Mediterranean basin, through trade in non-figurative goods (e.g. carpets, ceramics and silks). Whilst existing work already suggests that artistic exchange occurred in the medieval period, Mack extends the narrative by asserting that these artistic exchanges also occurred in Renaissance Italy. In doing so, Mack challenges the traditional view that Renaissance artistic achievements were a self-contained phenomenon. Thus, in Italy, a hybrid form of artistic production emerged but Mack does not view this as having hindered the cultural blossoming of either (western European or Ottoman) Renaissances. In fact, Mack concludes her book by writing, '[s]ixteenth century East–West trade and artistic exchange softened a clash of civilizations, establishing a historical precedent for cultural coexistence and mutual enrichment.'[48] This is a point firmly held by this study.

Luxury objects and their exchange certainly became part and parcel of elite and merchant life of both East and West. Both cultures depended on such exchange. In fact, trade was the life-blood of not only European life but of Mediterranean life more generally in the global Renaissance. It is this cultural coexistence that provided the fluidity of the Renaissance age and which demands a broader Renaissance purview. Such artistic and cultural exchanges—through diplomatic, commercial, and of course, military means—gave the Ottomans from the fifteenth century onwards the opportunities to be influenced not just by the legacy of the West but also by the classical heritage of the Islamic East. The impact of such exchanges influenced the visual expressions of its court culture beyond its borders in Eastern and Western Europe. Thus, the broader understanding of the Renaissance goes beyond the parameters of the Mediterranean and seeks to find a holistic explanation of the Ottoman Renaissance in the Ottoman's own meaningful context. Although important, the Ottoman Renaissance does not stop at the revival of ancient Greek and Roman ideals, or its interaction with the West. In response to an obvious lacuna in the literature, this essay explores explores the cultural, political and religious ties to the Ottomans' Eastern predecessors as well to demonstrate a larger context for the early modern Renaissance. Such an approach undermines the notion of *rinascita* and nineteenth-century Eurocentric perceptions of the age. By extending the contemporary historiographical discussion to previously excluded, yet intimately connected, others, the research uniquely highlights both the Eastern and Western legacy of the Ottoman Renaissance, and it brings to the fore the truly global nature of the early modern experience.

Indeed, the notion of an Ottoman Renaissance has been suggested before. Late nineteenth and early twentieth-century architectural historians acknowledged the notion of an Ottoman Renaissance in the fifteenth and sixteenth centuries. As early as 1874, German architect Friedrich Adler acknowledged the 'spatial unity' and 'purist character' of Ottoman architecture.[49] As early as 1907 the idea of a Turkish Renaissance emerged, initiated by the German art historian and architect Cornelius Gurlitt, who recognised the originality of Ottoman architecture and the creative genius of Sinan and placed both within the Renaissance paradigm.[50] Gurlitt in fact dismissed the common idea that Ottoman architecture was a mere imitation of the Hagia Sophia and recognised instead that it was a product of a shared Mediterranean legacy:

> We have been enthusiastic in our praise of Italy, a country that at the end of the fifteenth century resurrected the art of ancient Rome after this achievement had lain dormant for over a thousand years. During the same period, however, buildings were erected on the Bosphorus that have been belittled for the simple reason that they were replicas of Hagia Sophia. Yet it is no less a renaissance of astounding individuality that sprang up from the soil made fertile

> by the spirit of ancient Greece. The revival of ancient perceptions of shape and form occurred here with the same freedom, independence, and boldness, with the same artistic and creative force, that was shaping the culture on the opposite shores of the Adriatic Sea.[51]

Gurlitt argues that the sharing and fusing of cultural values shaped the sixteenth century cultural revivalism of the Mediterranean basin of which the Ottomans were also significant participants. The uniqueness of Gurlitt's early view of Ottoman art has only been taken up recently.

Building on the work of Cornelius Gurlitt, in 1914 the German orientalist Franz Babinger, in an article titled 'Die türkische Renaissance' (The Turkish Renaissance), compared Sinan's central plan domed mosques to the works of Bramante, Giuliano da Sangallo, Baldassare Peruzzi, and Michelangelo Buonarotti.[52] A year later Babinger even gave Sinan the sobriquet 'the Ottoman Michelangelo'.[53] The aim of his two articles was merely to invite historians and art historians to collaborate in bringing Sinan's works to universal recognition. His invitation was therefore like Necipoğlu's call for a 'fresh narrative'. Babinger recognised that Sinan's imperial architectural monuments and also the aesthetic decorative styles of Ottoman fine arts were products sparked by the same Renaissance spirit of curiosity and competitiveness that exemplified the period elsewhere in Europe.

By 1925 Glück, in collaboration with Ernest Diez, produced *Die Kunst des Islam* which further elaborated the theory of the Turkish Renaissance. Diez later argued that the Ottoman dynasty needed monumental 'architectural representation' like the Romans.[54] He went on to emphasise the cross-cultural heritage of Ottoman and Italian Renaissance architecture in the Roman imperial tradition and attributed their similarities to a 'period style'. He called this style '*Zeitstil*'.[55] Turkish historian Halil Inalcik who in 1973 published *The Ottoman Empire: The Classical Age 1300–1600* reached the same conclusion; that is, that the Ottoman imperial state architecture is not authentically Turkish but rather a product of past and present exemplars from Roman/Byzantine, Islamic, and Timurid-Persianate-Turkic traditions from Central Asia.[56] Furthermore, in 1986 art historian Esin Atıl concurred with the view that, like its architecture, Ottoman art of the fifteenth and sixteenth centuries 'saw the synthesis of European, Islamic and Turkish traditions and the creation of an artistic vocabulary that was unique to the Ottoman world'.[57] The result of a shared heritage by the Ottomans produced unique art mediums from the monumental religious to secular works of art including tiles, calligraphy, illustrated manuscripts, ceramics, carpets, and embroidered textiles. Combined with its ceremonials and pageants they reflected the power of the visual tastes of the sultan's court.

While Diez, Inalcık and Atıl argue that the Ottoman aesthetic is the product of a cultural fusion - this study goes further. It considers that at the core of the Ottoman aesthetic lay an underlying Renaissance mindset—one that was conscious of its historical legacy and global supremacy, and was determined to overcome the technological and engineering challenges it faced. With this conviction, visual representations of its ruling elite constructed a distinct early modern cultural identity through strategic imitation, adaptation and perfection (or surpassing) of their own cultural legacies. This distinct identity set the Ottoman aesthetic apart from its Eastern 'cousins'.

Despite some positive assessments of Ottoman art during the late nineteenth and early twentieth centuries, scholarly works produced in the latter decades of the twentieth century continued the ambivalent attitudes to early modern Ottoman achievements. Turkish architectural historian Doğan Kuban in his work *Ottoman Architecture* focuses on the functionality and practical aspects of Ottoman imperial mosques. While considering the complexity, architectural detail and workmanship, Kuban dismisses the notion that there was a rebirth in this area in the 15th and 16th centuries.[58] Further rejecting the Renaissance mindset of Sinan, one of his main claims is that treatises comparable to those in the West which set the standard for European architects, were not produced by Ottoman architects and other intellectuals in the East. Necipoğlu, however, finds this discourse very problematic because according to her 'it assumes that any kind of theoretical approach requires a Vitrivian written manifestation, whereas one can argue that, in Ottoman culture, certain aspects remained part of oral culture, and that written culture remained in a different manner'.[59] According to her this does not in any way prove that the Ottoman architects, including Sinan and other artisans, did not have a theory in mind. Other Ottoman architectural historians, including Godfrey Goodwin in his 1971 work *A History of Ottoman Architecture,* attempt to bring a balance to the debate. Goodwin states that the purpose of his work on Ottoman architecture is to demonstrate that 'far from being a merely a decadent mixture of Persian, Byzantine and other styles…' Ottoman architecture '… is a historic style in its own right.'[60] Although acknowledging the uniqueness of Ottoman art, Goodwin, like Kuban is also reluctant to engage in the notion of an early modern Ottoman Renaissance. Moreover, art historian Walter B. Denny, in his work *Iznik: The Artistry of Ottoman Ceramics,* asserts that the Ottomans made one of their greatest artistic contributions in early modern ceramic technology that 'reflected the fundamental design medium for Ottoman art.'[61] Atasoy and Atıl similarly affirm the creativity of early modern Ottoman fine arts.[62] It is at this point where this study builds on the previous works to bring to the fore the distinctive nature and character of the Ottoman Renaissance.

In her 2004 work, *Creating East and West: Renaissance Humanists and the Ottoman Turks,* in an epilogue entitled, 'The Renaissance Legacy', Nancy Bisaha acknowledges that Western views are still influenced by Renaissance humanist responses to the Ottoman Turks.[63] Despite the fact that Renaissance humanists cultivated a further understanding of Muslim culture and religion, they also fostered the 'hostile take on the Ottoman Turks', which 'only served to nurture incipient ideas of Western superiority to Eastern rivals'.[64] Indeed, Western historiography is still somewhat indecisive about the Ottomans, with scholars and academics still constrained by the traditionalist Renaissance legacy. They do not see the rebirth of Ottoman art on its own cultural merits. The core of this indecisiveness is seen by some as stemming from the centuries during which Europe faced the Ottoman threat.[65] As a consequence, the cultural expressions of the Ottomans were simply overlooked and not taken very seriously. Yet, there remain significant challenges to this viewpoint. For instance, Stephane Yerasimos states in relation to the Süleymaniye Mosque in Istanbul that '[i]t is interesting to observe how, in a mind as creative as Sinan's, an obsessive dialogue with a model can evolve into a path toward genuine originality'.[66] Art historians whose analyses have not taken account of his innovative style have misrepresented Sinan's mosque designs, which used a central dome flanked by two half-domes. According to Besnier-Kılıçoğlu, Sinan's 'failure to recognize the continuous development of syntactical conceptual methodology leads them to see the Süleymaniye Mosque as a copy of the sixth-century Byzantine basilica of Hagia Sophia'.[67] Rather than see his work as mere copies, many modern historians view Sinan's work as a meaningful fusion of Turkish and Byzantine elements, which together produce a distinctly Ottoman style. Instead, Sinan's distinctly early modern Ottoman style needs to be seen as one that 'perfects' the past exemplars and gives it rebirth in a new Ottoman cultural setting. In this way, his works are seen in the broader context of a growing empire, as complementing Ottoman expressions of ceremonial and political power, authority and universal legitimacy in an age where imperial rivalries in the Mediterranean competed with one another for regional and global supremacy.

Although Burckhardt's dream of a Renaissance civilisation in Italy has been revised by recent scholarship, Guido Ruggiero notes that the term Renaissance "seems continually to return, adapting itself to changing times'.[68] It is, therefore, natural to broaden the term beyond the confines of the Italo-centric narrative to include the Ottoman art of the early modern period. Indeed, by interrogating the Ottoman voices from the sixteenth-century historical context—Mustafa Ali and Sinan—the need for this broader understanding becomes even more apparent.

❧

The Ottoman Paradigm: Taqlid, tecdid, nezāket and zuhūrat in Ali's 'Epic Deeds of Artists'

In his work *Epic Deeds of Artists* (1587), Mustafa Ali provides an account of the lives of the artists of the East (that is, of the Muslim lands including the Ottoman world) and the part they played in the formulation of the fine arts in the sixteenth century. Unlike Vasari, Ali does not explicitly use the term 'rebirth' but instead conveys the idea through comparable expressions and sentiments. The Ottoman man of letters used terms such as *taqlid* (imitation) and *tecdid* (to make new, restore, or renovate) to describe early modern Ottoman cultural achievements, thereby reflecting the broader Mediterranean attitude to 'rebirth' discussed above.

Ali spent a year in Ottoman Baghdad from 1585 to 1586 as financial advisor to the Ottoman governor. The setting inspired in Ali a new worldview, which offered three significant insights into the idea of a political and cultural rebirth. First, from 750 to 1258 Baghdad served as the centre of the Abbasid Caliphate to which the Ottomans considered themselves heirs. Second, the Mongols destroyed the city in the thirteenth century and converted to Islam. They then became the champions of Islamic civilisation through their descendants—the Timurids—to whom Ali recognises Ottoman ethnic connections. Third, the collapse of the Mongol Khans from the mid-fourteenth century and the rise of the nomadic Turkic tribes from the steppes, created a new political context which according to Fleischer:

> [...] is marked by a process of amalgamation between the political ideals of the steppe and the sedentary values and institutions of the Irano-Islamic high cultural traditions to which the conquerors had fallen heir by confession.[69]

Here, Ali's acknowledgement of the triumph of the Turkic tribes after their conversion to Islam serves as another factor in the way the past shapes the present. As an historian, Ali was able to see the achievements of the Ottomans through their cultural ownership of their past Eastern legacies. In this way, the past for Ali served as a signpost to make sense of the sixteenth century Ottoman world.

Ali's sojourn in Baghdad enabled him to formulate his understanding of Ottoman cultural and artistic achievements in his time. He observed how the Ottomans absorbed and adapted both the visual aesthetics and learning from the medieval Islamic civilisation of the Abbasids, the Timurid efflorescence, and the political ideologies of the steppe heritage. Despite the devastation it had suffered at the hands of the Mongols three centuries earlier, sixteenth-century Baghdad continued to attract an array of visitors from merchants to philosophers from the East. This reflected its cosmopolitan makeup as a city where sharing ideas and developing new ones once again recalled the heyday of its medieval glory.

Furthermore, Ottoman Baghdad gave Mustafa Ali an opportunity to be at the centre of Islamic medieval knowledge. In the West, Vasari turned to,

> [...] notes and memoranda, which I had prepared ever from my boyhood, for my own recreation, and because of a certain affection which I preserved toward the memory of our artists, every notice respecting whom had always been most interesting to me.[70]

In the same way, Ali was in a unique position to scan the entire Islamic world—from Herat in the east, to Safavid Persia and Egypt, the Arab worlds, and his own artists of Rum (i.e. Ottoman) in the west. He had the opportunity to immerse himself in the artistic and intellectual Persianate milieu and Safavid culture. He observed the rich interconnections and legacies forged there.[71] He could converse with storytellers like Yazdi, and Qutb al-din a composer of biographical treatise on calligraphers and painters, a copy of which Ali read during his service there.[72] Indeed, like Vasari, his impressions were recorded in a text specifically focused on the artists: *The Epic Deeds of Artists* (1587).

Like Vasari, Ali had first-hand knowledge of the artists he wrote about. Communicating with peers, enthusiasts, local and other Muslim artists about the artistic world of the East, and consulting the written sources that he had collected over a period of time allowed him to compose his own art treatise. This work not only showed the achievements of Muslim artists, but more importantly emphasised the successes of the Ottoman artists particularly.

As a literary source, *Epic Deeds of Artists* is composed in Ottoman Turkish with Persian and Arabic interspersed throughout. Ali demonstrates his full grasp and appreciation of this literary genre. Like Vasari, one of Ali's goals in composing this work was to create an uninterrupted linear progress (*silsile-i celileye ihtisasla*) in the history of Muslim art, which he understood to be an integral part of a civilisation's progress.[73] Such an understanding would enable him to construct his framework for Ottoman cultural rebirth. In his text, Ali recounts the lives of about 270 Muslim artists, beginning with the third century Chinese painter Mani (216–274 CE) before jumping into the Islamic period. He ends his treatise by praising the achievements of Ottoman painting from the contemporary Ottoman court painter Nakkaş Osman (d. 1600?) who worked in the ateliers of Murad III.

As an art historical treatise one of the drawbacks of *Epic Deeds of Artists* is that, unlike Vasari, Ali does not establish any set criteria against which to make judgements on style. By providing the reader with information only on the origins, personalities, and virtues of the artists, his discussion about their art is limited. The constraints of Ali's approach make interpretation of his art treatise problematic, as his message is not always clear. He does, however, make some broad references to the main area of the artists' specialisations, such as Master Uthman's (i.e. Nakkaş Osman's) fascination with detail in *şebih* (human portraiture), or Şah Kulu's mastery in the *saz* style of serrated leaves. But Ali does not develop an account of their specific themes or individual works. Ali's omission of architecture and ceramics from the treatise weakens his work, limiting its claim to be a true representation of Ottoman fine arts.

Other limitations in Ali's treatise lie in his visual analysis and in the structure of the text. His analysis of the originality of art works is problematic. Without establishing any set criteria, he uses ambiguous terms like 'original', 'pleasing styles', 'inimitable' and 'impeccable' to describe artistic achievements. Additionally, he devotes four out of five chapters of the text to the art of calligraphy and merely one to painting. Clearly, such an arrangement signifies his bias towards the art of writing of which he was a master. As God's Word was recorded in the Qu'ran, text was much more highly prized in art than was imagery, with calligraphy indeed becoming the most sacred of art forms.[74] However, despite its limitations, *Epic Deeds of Artists* is the only existing text from which we can learn about the sixteenth-century Ottoman attitude to the arts, and for this reason alone it is an essential source for this study.

Ali stresses the point that his main objective in *Epic Deeds of Artists* is to promote the art and artists of Rum (that is, the Ottomans). Just as Vasari saw that it was his 'genius' to recognise the need to record for posterity the Tuscan patrimony of art, Ali also wished to publicise new works by lesser-known artists. In so doing, Ali's focus turns almost exclusively to the East. He makes comparisons between Turkic and Central Asian Timurid–Persian artists' styles and those of the Ottomans to reinforce the Eastern influence on the nature of Ottoman cultural expression. Just as the Tuscan vision of rebirth looked to Greece and Rome, the Ottoman orientation towards the East defined its Renaissance. Ali provides an insight into the practices of a culturally dynamic and creative international atmosphere by including the foreign artists from the East working in conjunction with the local *nakkashane* (atelier) masters at the palace ateliers.[75] For Ali, this international collaboration of artistic activity at the Topkapı Palace, as well as in Bursa and Edirne from 1413 onward, contributed to producing works that stylistically became synonymous with early modern Ottoman visual expressions. Ali's emphasis on the East suggests that modern day Renaissance scholars need to do the same.

Unlike Vasari, Ali does not explicitly refer to 'rebirth'; instead, he implies it. Like Vasari's emphasis on *imitazione, adeguazione* and *perfezione* Ali, too praises those artists who resort to *taqlid* (imitation), *tecdid* (restoration), and *nezāket* (refinement) of artworks to attain *zuhūrat* (perfection). His inclusion of Eastern artists in *Epic Deeds of Artists* who flourished during the Timurid Renaissance from Samarkand to Herat, and Tabriz to Bursa at the time and after Timur's incursions into Anatolia is crucial. Ali suggests that the Timurid achievements found perfection in his own time through the patronage of the Ottoman sultans.[76] Ottomans are historically and ethnically connected to these cultural accomplishments of their brothers in the East and in his biased tone, like Vasari, Ali elevates the Ottoman achievements in his own time as being superior to the past and present exemplars. He speaks of Ottomans mastering previous Persian calligraphic styles by way of *taqlid* and creating a distinctly Ottoman calligraphic mode by *nezāket* or refining the original script in form and style.[77] In the fine arts of illumination as well as book repair, Ali speaks of 'Monla Sharaf of Yazd [d.1454] [who] was his time's outstanding master of excellent refinement'.[78] In the area of gold sprinkling Qadi Ahmed was 'a remarkable master'.[79] For Ali it is through *taqlid, tecdid* and *nezāket* that the arts of old are brought back to life, renewed and perfected in a new and original form or *sūret*.[80] Ali praises 'men of refinement and learning' who, with their craft of calligraphy, 'embellish the pages of time', restoring and repairing past works.[81] He highlights that, by learning from the past, 'men of refinement' perfect or *zuhūrat* the art of the Word through their 'elegant penmanship' or *qat'-i qalem ve nezāket -i raqam*.[82]

Ali's analysis of the rebirth of calligraphy begins with the thirteenth century chief calligrapher of the Abbasid court, Yaqut al-Musta'simi (d. 1298). Ali praises Yaqut al-Musta'simi for giving rebirth to the esteemed profession by perfecting the art form, writing *Yaqut zuhūr eyledi* (Yaqut perfected it.)[83] While the original *kufic* art of calligraphy had not been forgotten since the earliest recording of the Qur'an in the late seventh to early eighth centuries, Ali emphasises that it had become stifled and in need of rejuvenation. He makes this point clear in his analysis underscoring the linear progression (*silsile-i celileye ihtisasla*) of stylistic development:

> It was Ibn Muqla [886-940] who first Arabicized the *Kufic* style, then Ibn a-Bawwab [d.1022] refined it, and then Yaqut al-Musta'simi [d.1298] perfected it and he standardized it by listing all its regulations.[84]

This is the closest Ali comes to paralleling the Vasarian discourse in implying the *ihya* or rebirth of calligraphy through a progression of historical figures. Also like Vasari, Ali recognises the importance of past art forms and addresses their significance to the progress of a civilisation. He acknowledges the ninth century Ibn Muqla for creating a sense of cultural and unified religious consciousness by 'Arabicizing' the original *kufic* style. A century later the *kufic* style was further refined, *i'rab* (made clear) by Ibn Bawwab. Yaqut's style was emulated and modified by calligraphers for centuries to come. Ali mentions Yaqut's 'pearls of rules of calligraphy' having been reborn by the master: *usūl* (fundamentals), *terkīb* (ligatures), *kurrās* (support), *nisbet* (i.e. interrelation or harmony of design in relation of the script to the white space), *su'ūd* (upstroke) and *teşmir* (extension), *nüzūl* (down-stroke) and *irsāl* (flourish).[85] Like Vasari's veneration of Tuscan artists, Ali extols the artists of Rum (i.e. the Ottomans) for their *taqlid* and *tecdid*. He acknowledges that their innovations on early Persian models ultimately bring in new '*ihtira sūret*' (original forms or style).[86]

Ali skips a few centuries to bring his discussion up to the achievements of the Ottomans in his own time. One needs to be aware of his exclusive narrative which prioritises Ottoman greatness against the other Eastern accomplishments. He praises the progress made in this esteemed art form of calligraphy during the fifteenth and sixteenth centuries at the Topkapı Palace by the calligraphers Sheyh Hamdullah (1436–1520), Ahmed Karahısarı (1486–1556) and Hasan Karahısarı. The Ottomans' modifications of the canonical script used for religious works of art meant looking back to their past heritage to create their own distinct *Ottoman ta'liq* style. According to Rogers and Ward this style 'had been developed in the Timurid court of Tabriz, Shiraz and

Herat in the early fifteenth century' and became a favoured style at the court of Süleyman the Magnificent.[87]

Sheyh Hamdullah's copies of the Qur'an transformed the rounded scripts to Ottoman taste. Ottoman calligraphers learnt from precedents like that of Yaqut's 1282–83 Qur'anic verse decorated in sixteenth century Ottoman illumination, written in the *muhaqqaq* style and housed at the Topkapı Palace. Such works provided the likes of Sheyh Hamdullah with a prototype that marked the revival of the art of Turkish calligraphy *(Figures 1and 2)*. He became the first Ottoman calligrapher to consolidate the canonical Arabic 'six scripts' that calligraphers are required to employ in the copying of the Qur'an. This principle, established by Yaqut al-Musta'simi, meant introducing additional new styles *nasta'liq, jele, nesih, kufi, tevki, divani, jele-talik, jele-divani, jele-thuluth* as seen in Figure 2 of Sheyh Hamdullah's 'Murakka Calligraphic Album' at the Museum of Turkish and Islamic Arts in Istanbul.[88] These new styles were combined with the *nezāket* (refinement) of the art of *tughra,* which by the sixteenth century had become the distinctive Ottoman symbol of the religious and secular power and authority of the sultan. Together, these developments marked the epitome and surpassing of the past precedents in a uniquely Ottoman calligraphic *sūret* (style).

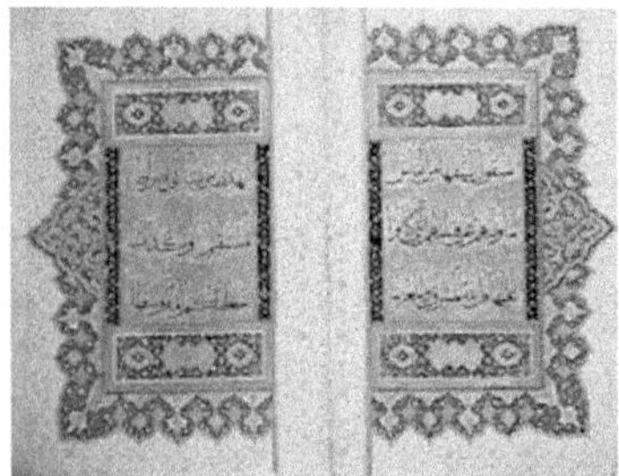

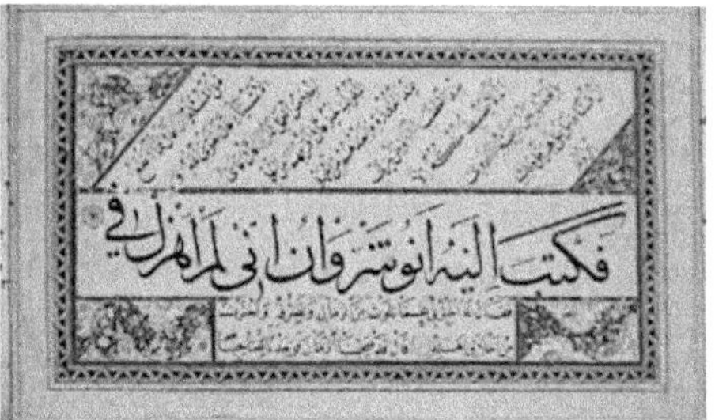

Figures 1, 2. Left, a Qur'an page from Yaqut al-Musta'simi (1282–1283); right, pages from 15th century Sheyh Hamdullah's album. Photograph reproductions.

The art of *tughra* in particular continued to evolve artistically with each subsequent sultan signifying both his religious and secular fashioning. At Sheyh Hamdullah's death, Ali wrote the following panegyric:

> Ever since the calligraphy of Hamdi son of Shaykh appeared. The writings of Yaqut has surely vanished from the world.[89]

This verse reflects the Ottoman refinement of the art form from previous eras.[90] This reinforces Ali's acknowledgement of the progression and development of the art of calligraphy, not only in book form as with the copies of the Qur'an, but also as decorative artwork in mosque architecture.

Ali mentions two figures who excelled in the use of calligraphy as an art form in mosque interior decorative arts: Ahmed Karahısarı's (1486–1556) calligraphic works in the Süleymaniye Mosque (1557–58), and his adopted son Hasan Karahısarı's artistry in the Selimiye Mosque (1575). According to Sinan's autobiographies Hasan Karahısarı 'became a second Yaqut in the world', implying the attainment of an equivalent 'high Renaissance period' in Ottoman–Turkish calligraphy under the patronage of the Ottoman sultan.[91] As a calligrapher, Ali's bias for this art form dominates all others. For Ali, the *thuluth* inscriptions of Ahmed Karahısarı on the domes of Sinan's mosques are 'The glory of [the art of] of writing'. [92] By this description he implies that the Ottoman master has surpassed the thirteenth century Abbasid calligrapher Yaqut al-Must'asimi and attained the ideal of perfection at the court of Süleyman the Magnificent (*Figures 3 and 4*). With the monumental inscriptions introduced in imperial mosque architecture by Ahmed and Hasan Karahısarı, the art of calligraphy reached new heights. Structurally, by placing the Ottoman achievements at the end of his work, Ali is symbolically situating them as the inheritors of all those artists who came before. In this way he, like Vasari, boasts of the attainment of the perfection of the arts under Ottoman patronage in his own time.

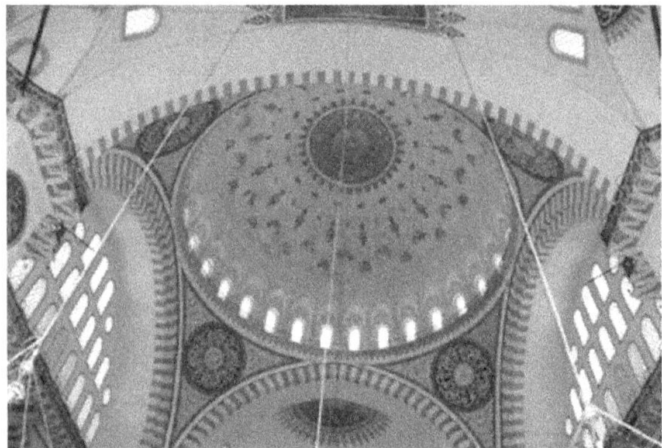
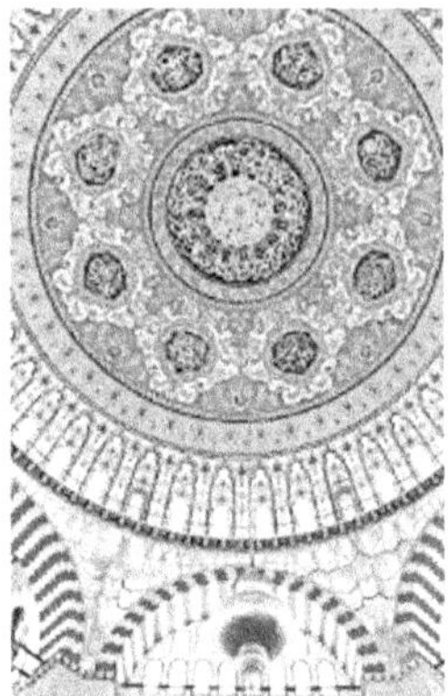

Figures 3, 4. Left, the central dome of the Süleymaniye Mosque 1557, Istanbul; right, the central dome of the Selimiye Mosque 1575, Edirne claimed by Sinan to have surpassed the dome of the Hagia Sophia. Photographs by Metin Mustafa, December 4, 2014.

While calligraphy dominates four out of five chapters of the art treatise, the art of painting is covered in the last section of Ali's work. His brief descriptions of painters make it difficult for art historians to reach an accurate assessment of Ali's intentions. Focusing on Persian, Timurid and Ottoman painters from the fifteenth to the sixteenth centuries, Ali ends his chapter by praising the Ottoman artist Nakkaş Osman for his portraits of the sultans at the court of Murad III. He emphasises Osman's fascination with detail in *şebih* (human portraiture), or Şah Kulu's mastery in the *saz* style of serrated leaves. Ali does not develop an account of their specific themes or individual works. Ali's omission of architecture and ceramics from the treatise weakens his work, limiting its claim to be a true representation of Ottoman fine arts.

In his assessment of Ottoman style and rebirth Ali does not ignore the contribution of Italian artists or style on the Ottomans. He recognises the achievements of past palace artists from the time of Mehmed II, Süleyman the Magnificent, and Murad III, including the fifteenth-century painter Sinan Bey, 'who appeared at the paradise resembling palace (harem)' as the portrait painter of Sultan Mehmed II.[93] He acknowledges that Sinan Bey was a pupil of a 'Frankish master named

Mastor [Maestro] Paoli who flourished in Venice and became a most exalted artist in his field'. [94] Mustafa Ali also includes in his praises Sinan's pupil Shibilzada Ahmed, a 'native of Bursa', although Gülru Necipoğlu acknowledges Costanzo da Ferrara as his master *(Figure 5).*[95] Figure 5 is the only three-quarter profile of Mehmed II and is attributed to either Sinan Bey or Ahmed Shibilzada of Bursa. The picture clearly demonstrates Italian Renaissance influence. Such a larger than life representation of any figure had never been attempted before by any Ottoman painter. Although Ali provides only brief statements, his acknowledgement of the contributions of the Western masters to the Ottoman artistic *oeuvre* clearly advocates looking beyond the East to create something new and unique in the Ottoman art tradition.

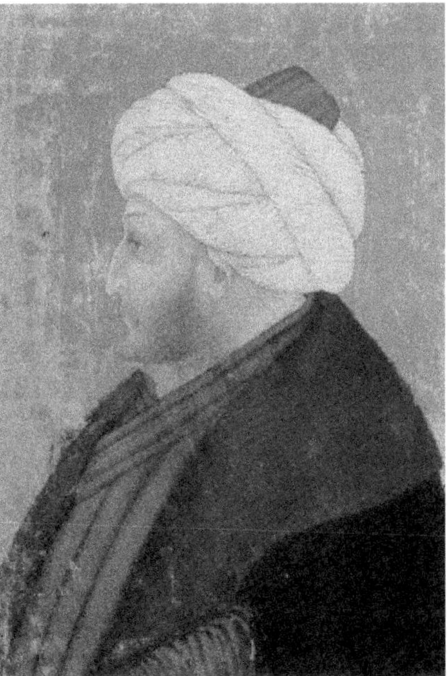

Figure 5. Three-quarter-profile portrait of Mehmed II, attributed to either Sinan Bey or Sibilzade Ahmed of Bursa, c.1480. Photograph reproduction.

Furthermore, the transference of the legacy of the West to the Ottoman artistic *oeuvre* reinforces the cultural interaction in the Mediterranean basin, prompting a sharing of ideas. Ali mentions:

> ...the talented Re'is Haydar ... known as Naqqas Haydar or Nigari, he was a person whose artistry and talent in human portraiture, especially in depicting the portrait of the late Sultan Selim (II).[96]

Nigari was a portrait artist from the middle of the sixteenth century in the tradition of Sinan Bey who had been trained by the Venetian Gentile Bellini a century earlier. His paintings became available to Italian artists.[97] In his portraits of Sultan Süleyman and one of two portraits of Selim II, for example, Nigari's Western influence is seen in his use of techniques of shading which he clearly learned from European art, and his figures are always set against a dark background (*Figures 6 and 7*). His figures are posed in a style evocative of both the Islamic miniature painting traditions and European-style portraiture. His depiction of Süleyman, especially in his old age, in unpretentious attire, strolling in a garden accompanied by his attendants, standing alone, lost in thought, his back bent and, face lined and gaunt is emotionally moving, and representative of the monarch's ill health in his latter life and the burden of his responsibilities.

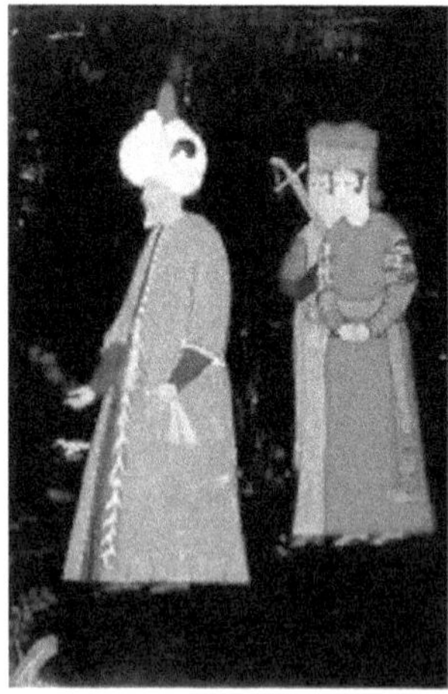

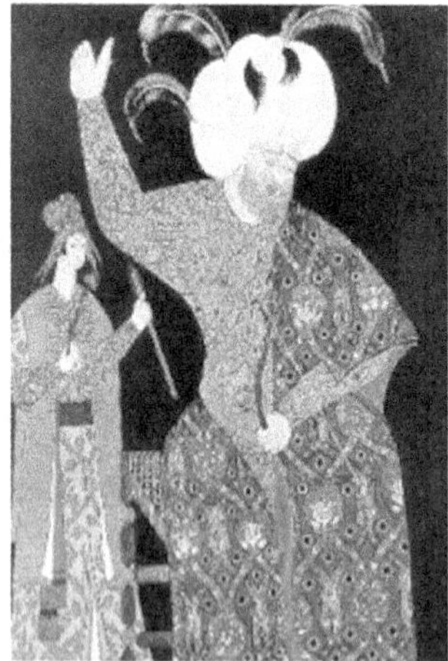

Figures 6, 7. Left, the ageing Sultan Süleyman with his attendants; right, Selim II, by Nigari c.1560–65. Photograph reproductions.

The physical availability of Nigari's work to Italian and French artists makes this cultural exchange even more pertinent because it reflects the humanist interest of coming to terms with one's mortality irrespective of status. For Ali, the training provided by Bellini and others represents a shared cultural heritage where the transmission of classical Western modes to Ottoman portraiture creates authoritative guidelines recognisable to both East and West. This cultural exchange equally demonstrates the indirect access to the classicism of the Western Roman Empire the Ottomans had without compromising their cultural ideals.

Perceiving Ottoman rebirth as an integral part of a shared cultural heritage, past inter-cultural connections makes Ali's notion of Ottoman artistic achievements unique. With his vision firmly set on the East, Ali provides twenty-first century scholars with a broader historical framework and an alternative paradigm from which to revise the Renaissance discourse—one that breaks from the orientalist perspective and integrates the east into the narrative. More significantly in the context of this discussion, however, Ali's reference to the transmission of the art of painting from West to East contributes to the broader legacy of the classical arts while adapting the Islamic–Turkic *sūret* and giving it its own unique *ihya* (rebirth) with a distinctly Ottoman flavour, as seen in the sitting pose and the bent knees of the sultan in *Mehmed II Smelling a Rose* (*Figure 8*). Finally, in keeping with Jörn Rüsen's idea, Ali demonstrates that:

> [h]istorical consciousness belongs to the elementary cultural achievements of his life, through which he organises his temporality for and through himself, the objective and the subjective, through which internal and external time are brought into equilibrium, that enable man to interact as a being directed at the future and influenced by experience, with his world and himself.[98]

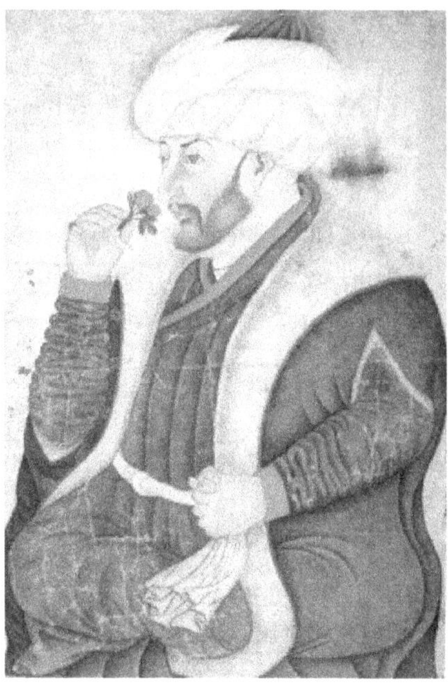

Figure 8. Mehmed II Smelling a Rose, attributed to Sinan Bey, trained by Gentile Bellini at the Topkapı Palace. Photograph reproduction.

In short, Ali's experience at Baghdad provided him with the intellectual understanding to bring into 'equilibrium' the linear progression of past and present, thereby offering a contextual understanding of the Ottoman artistic experiences as a new cultural rebirth. Although Ali notes this understanding only very briefly in reviewing stylistic development in the history of painting in the Ottoman court, he does, however, confirm the spirit of the rebirth of Ottoman arts. While Ali's sentiments of Ottoman rebirth in the art of painting may be limited in comparison to his discussion of calligraphy, his omission of architecture entirely in *Epic Deeds of Artists* is quite problematic. This is where the imperial architect Sinan's *Treatise on Architecture* fills the gap.

The Ottoman Paradigm: Sinan's 'azim (magnificence)

According to Madison, cultural appropriation 'involves an intertextual process of creating or revisioning an object, idea, or subject from another object, idea, or subject to create another or different version.'[99] Cultural appropriation does not intend to imitate or mimic 'or to necessarily make it known that appropriation has even taken place or to reveal that in creating this new form something has been borrowed'.[100] In the Ottoman architectural context, the sixteenth-century imperial architect Sinan boastfully states in his autobiographies that he triumphed over the Roman/Byzantine Hagia Sophia by creating the largest dome the world had ever seen at the time, clearly demonstrating the Ottoman competitive spirit of the age and the creation of a new distinct art medium.[101]

Like his Renaissance contemporaries, Sinan composed his treatise '...in order that a memorial and record [of his artworks] endure through the pages of time.'[102] The treatise lists all his works—mosques, hospices, madrasas, bridges, palaces, fountains and countless other structures—as a testimony of the decades of learning and adapting of the old into something new in the creation of a distinct Ottoman style. Sinan states:

> I acquired a sought-after bit of wisdom from the crenellation of great ancient remains and a provision of knowledge from every ruined monument.[103]

Having learned from the ancient ruins around him by *tecdid* (restoring, renovating and renewing), he refined his *sūret, üsl'ub* (style) and gave rebirth to the old.[104] Sinan attained *'azim* (magnificence), *nezāket* (elegance, refinement), *cemile* (beauty) and *zuhūrat*, literally meaning perfection, through a rebirth of stylistic progression in his buildings leading to his distinct new *sūret*.[105] Like Vasari and Ali, Sinan saw a linear progress in his work. 'Day by day many types of buildings being created, and refinement increased', he writes, signifying the progression of art through the ages and culminating in 'art attain[ing] complete realization.'[106] Praising his 1548 work of adapting the Hagia Sophia model with his style in the Şehzade Mosque in Istanbul, Sinan confirms, 'such artistry had not been previously accomplished by any master' because previous works imitating the *Ayasōfya tarzı[nda]* (Hagia Sophia style) structure 'did not possess elegance'.[107] Sinan informs the reader that the Roman/Byzantine structure of the Ayasōfya *tarzı[nda]* became the inspiration for his works and that these works in return became a *nūmūne* (model) for the Süleymaniye Mosque (1557–8):

> [...] this servant perfected the noble Friday mosque of Şehzade Sultan Mehmed ... in the style of Hagia Sophia ... which was the model for the model building complex of His Majesty Sultan Süleyman Khan.[108]

To signify the rebirth of the classical past with the present exemplified in the Süleymaniye Mosque, Sinan refers to 'four marble columns' used in the construction of the building.[109] Like St Peter's 'stone columns' coming from Roman antiquity 'the mold of Hadrian' according to Vasari, each of Sinan's four marble columns came from different parts of the empire.[110] He states:

Each of its variegated marbles was removed to the horizon and came as a token from a different land. According to most historians they were left from the palace of His Majesty Solomon's Belkis [Queen of Sheba] ... Also another brought from Alexandria with a base ... another column [i.e. from the remnants of the old Byzantine Palace] was found standing ready in the imperial palace [Topkapı Palace], [and the] Maiden's Column [from the Church of the Holy Apostles in Istanbul].[111]

The symbolism surely was not lost on the patron. The columns alluded to the Biblical Solomon, the namesake of Sultan Süleyman, ancient Egypt, the Eastern Roman emperors, and Christianity, demonstrating the Ottoman dominance of these civilisations under Süleyman.

According to Selen B. Morkoç, the use of the marble columns from Istanbul and other parts of the empire allude to "[...] distinct royal connotations even if they appeared to be identical'.[112] Combined with the Hagia Sophia style, this gave rebirth to the classical past within an Islamic monument that embraced all the civilisations that came before it, allowing Sinan to claim, 'The arts manifested in it.'[113] Under his guidance the old model of the Hagia Sophia was transformed into a distinctly new Ottoman form in the Süleymaniye and embodied the '*azim*' of Ottoman cultural greatness.

Sinan's self-aggrandising tone in relation to his achievement in the Süleymaniye is reflective of the Renaissance spirit of the age. It also embodies his claim that such monumental representation was a true reflection of a global ruler like Süleyman. As Lowenthal exclaims, '[a] magnified or invented antiquity also aggrandizes localities and individuals'.[114] The visual metaphor of the Süleymaniye Mosque had definitely established the universal status of Süleyman, while the city of Istanbul gained the crowning glory of Ottoman imperialism. Necipoğlu asserts that the complex '[...] demonstrate[s] that culturally recognized symbolic and ideological [political and religious] associations ... constitute[s] a significant aspect of the Süleymaniye's multi-layered architectural discourse'.[115] By resurrecting these four columns of antiquity within the context of the sixteenth century, Sinan emphasises the nature of Ottoman historical consciousness. For Sinan, the structure makes sense of the Ottoman cultural rebirth through the convergence of Roman/Byzantine with the Islamic-Timurid-Perso-Turkic historical memory with the creation of the new in the present. This understanding resonates with Jörn Rüsen's theory of the lasting legacy of historical consciousness:

> Historical consciousness specifically does not reduce the meaningful and sense bearing time to just the past, rather ... historical memory will always and fundamentally have a perspective of the present and the future. [116]

Vasari had noted that Florentine artists in 1013 learnt from the ancients works by imitating 'the good ancient order in the doors, windows, columns, arches and cornices, which they perceived in part in the very ancient church of San Giovanni'[117] before their art reached its status of *perfezione*, that is, its 'great' and 'truly extraordinary beauty' with Michelangelo. Similarly, Sinan, like his Italian Renaissance counterpart, attained *'azim* (magnificence), *nezāket* (elegance, refinement), *cemile* (beauty). Each of his art works—mosques, minarets, mihrabs, minbars, fountains—were like the Tuscan creations 'each of them matchlessly furnished' and 'attained perfection' that had developed since the days of the Abbasids signifying the Ottoman rebirth.[118]

This attainment of *'azim* reflects strongly the humanist influence of ancient Greece on the Ottomans. The idea of magnificence, imbued in the architecture of Sinan, aligns with Aristotelian notions of magnificence expressed in the *Nicomachean Ethics*. Here, 'the greatness implied in the name of the magnificent man ... will produce a more magnificent work of art.'[119] Like Aristotle's notion of magnificence, Sinan's *'azim'* also acquires an aesthetic dimension.

Furthermore, Sinan expressed his Sufi ideals in his esoteric work in the Rustem Pasha Mosque (1560–61) through the use of floral naturalism of Iznik tiles. By 1575 the rebirth of the classical arts enabled the Ottomans to *a'zam* (surpass) the past and declare to the world a high Renaissance building in the Selimiye Mosque:

> Never would a dome like Hagia Sophia's be built, the world wagered. This exalted dome exceeded that [and this mosque] is worthy of the admiration of humankind.[120]

For Sinan, this state of *zuhūrat* (perfection) and *a'zam* (surpassing) through rebirth came to fruition in his own lifetime under his artistic guidance, recalling Vasari's claim that (European) art reached perfection in his own time.

Sinan's dialogue with the sixth-century Roman/Byzantine Hagia Sophia resonates throughout his *Treatise on Architecture.* The references to Ayasōfya suggests that Sinan was a man of intellect and one of curiosity who not only studied this building closely throughout his career as the imperial architect of the empire but who restored it (*tecdid*), gave rebirth to it to strengthen the massive dome on the orders of Selim II in 1572–73 to prevent it from collapsing.[121] In his autobiography Sinan states that 'a few years after its completion, the dome collapsed' but was later 'rebuilt by the ... architect–engineer with various apologies'.[122] The significance here in Sinan's assessment of the quality of ancient works is that although they are worthy to be studied and emulated, they are not without defect.[123] For the purposes of this study, the implications of the choice of words used in Ottoman–Turkish by Sultan Selim II and Sinan are significant. The words *ihya, tecdid* and *zuhūrat* literally translate as 'rebirth', 'bringing back to life anew', 'restoring', 'resurrecting', and finally bringing something original into existence through perfection.[124] With the transformation of the Hagia Sophia into a distinctly Ottoman–Islamic monument, its Christian origins dissipated. It was reborn in the new form. This important project, however, is omitted from Sinan's autobiographies. Although he does not specifically use the word *ihya* in his work, one does, however, learn of the court's intentions from imperial edicts addressed to Sinan personally. The sixteenth century historian Selaniki notes that the Sultan was informed of the building's (i.e. Hagia Sophia) structural weakness and of its imminent collapse.[125] Sultan Selim II therefore issued an order:

> It is my request to give rebirth to the noble Friday mosque as my own imperial monument.[126]

The sultan's *firman* or edict orders a massive renovation project that involves strengthening the buttresses and building a minaret on one of them. Selaniki informs us that the Hagia Sophia has not witnessed such *ihya* (rebirth) in more than a millennium. Most significantly, however, is that the formal imperial ownership of the new Ottomanised Hagia Sophia by the sultan solidifies the Ottomans' legitimacy as the 'true' heirs to the Eastern Roman legacy. Changes began with Mehmed II's, Selim I's and Süleyman's single minaret additions to the structure. Now Selim II's fourth minaret gave Justinian's building its present look. Just as 'Michelagnolo had given life to the building [i.e. St Peter's]' as noted by Vasari, similarly Sinan too has given life to the Hagia Sophia 'which is there at the present day'.[127] Combined with its internal Islamic additions of a *mihrab, minbar,* and sultan's loge, the transformation of the Christian Hagia Sophia into an Islamic building was complete.

This project as well as Sinan's work on previous buildings in the Hagia Sophia style constituted a learning process from the ancient structures. At the hands of Ottoman artisans, the Hagia Sophia underwent many renovations:

> building a minaret above the reinforcement ... building [new] buttresses and water channels in the thirty-five-cubit-wide open space, repairing ... all necessary places at the interior and exterior ... reusing ... stones and bricks for the renovation of essential places.[128]

This reborn building is celebrated in c.1581 watercolour on paper from Seyyid Lokman's *Şahname-i Salim Khan* with new Ottoman additions including the mausoleum of Selim II on the sacred grounds.[129] Furthermore, folio 190b of the 1582 miniature painting in the *Surname-i Humayun* manuscript depicts a model of the Süleymaniye mosque paraded in front of Sultan Murad III. The model of the Süleymaniye carried by Sinan himself reflects the Ottoman Renaissance attitude of cultural greatness in the Süleymanic Age in the latter decades of the sixteenth century. This suggests that Ottoman artists eventually ceased using Hagia Sophia—which had long dominated the discourse until the building of the Süleymaniye—for their architectural inspiration. Instead, they created their own original and creative masterpieces. The float of the Süleymaniye dominates the entire folio 190b, signifying this shift in Ottoman architectural vision for the future architectural aesthetic.[130] By this stage, Sinan's distinctive architectural style had entered the consciousness of Ottoman art, signalling its confidence in its own cultural achievements; at this point, the past was left behind because it had done its job to define and shape its present.

Oleg Grabar in *The Formation of Islamic Art* acknowledges that Islamic cultural appropriation of past exemplars demonstrate 'the conscious attempt to relate meaningfully to the conquered word, by Islamicizing forms and ideas of old'.[131] According to Grabar, cultural appropriation for Islam was important to demonstrate its dominance as a burgeoning culture and religion by taking aspects of older cultures and making them *Islamic*.[132] By appropriating the historic and religious significance of the site of the Dome of the Rock in Jerusalem, and borrowing motifs from Sassanians and Byzantines in its decorative aesthetics, Grabar argues that Muslim architects created a monument that not only demonstrated Islam's political permanence in the region but also its religious and cultural.[133]

Furthermore, Ottoman restoration of ancient Islamic sites reinforced the notion of rebirth. Beginning with Süleyman and continuing into the reigns of his son Selim II and grandson Murad III, the three Holy Sites of Islam, Mecca, Medina and Jerusalem underwent massive restorations. Overseeing the restoration of the ancient Islamic site of the Ka'ba in Mecca, Sinan reflects the Ottomans' ongoing dialogue in mediating between two classical civilisations. In 1551 he 'repaired the defects of ... the Ka'ba' (*tecdid etmiş*).[134] Twenty years later he restored the Holy Shrine, the Ka'ba in Mecca 1571–84 'according to its old form' suggested by the decree of Sultan Selim II.[135] This signifies the bringing back to life of the legacy of this ancient Holy House with some Ottoman refinements or *nezāket*. Like the Hagia Sophia, the Ka'ba had not been revitalised since the Umayyad renovations of 693 by Caliph Abdul Malik bin Marwan, pitting the Ottomans in direct association with the past. Beginning with construction of the dilapidated roofs of the Haram [i.e. Holy Precinct], the Ottoman artisans added minarets, created a domical arcade with 360 domes around the Ka'ba, supported by new stone pillars.[136] According to Necipoğlu:

> Since the old foundations were incapable of bearing the load of stone domes, new foundations were laid ... [where] these domical arcades visually Ottomanised the Haram.[137]

By Ottomanising the holiest site of Islam, the Ottoman sultans were also legitimising their caliph-status in the Muslim world.

Like Vasari, the sole purpose of both Ali's and Sinan's works is to promote the arts of the Ottoman world. Ali's self-aggrandising endorsement reflects the achievements and successes of Ottoman artists over their Eastern counterparts. Similarly, with their predominantly boastful tone, Sinan's autobiographies promote a lasting legacy for all time where his works will be the subject of much discussion and admiration. His tendency to boast about his architectural achievements and decorative aesthetics led him to claim that he had created 'magnificent' (*'azim*) works of art by studying and learning from past exemplars. Like Vasari's elevation of Tuscan artists above others, Sinan's boasts work to promote his achievements over that of his contemporaries as well as his precursors.

CONCLUSION

In conclusion, through the works of Ali and Sinan the sixteenth century understanding of Ottoman notion of rebirth emerges. This understanding clearly expresses a sense of Ottoman historical consciousness and identity in an expanding empire which sees its cultural rebirth as part of the self-fashioning of its worldview. For Vasari's Ottoman contemporaries, rebirth coincided with a political impetus mediating between East and West. In his political history *Essence of History*, Ali connects the Ottomans' eastern heritage and the Turco–Mongol, Timurid, Persian, and Islamic elements and sees these as signalling the Ottoman's dynastic and religious legitimacy over the Muslim world. Ali's analysis demonstrates that, for the Ottomans, looking to the past meant making sense of their cultural revival within the context of universal sovereignty. This legitimacy demonstrated through art is enunciated in Ali's art treatise *Epic Deeds of Artists.* Ali's notion of Ottoman artistic rebirth converges with Vasarian views of *rinascita,* where stylistic evolution from past exemplars helps shape progress made in the present. This reinforces the Vasarian idea of the Tuscan *rinascita* as 'seeing past events as present'.[138] Calligraphic works and paintings from Abbasid and Persian exemplars, together with European interactions, led to a sharing of values and ideas. This interaction prompted the Ottoman artists to create new styles (*ihtirā sūret*) through *nezāket* (refinement) and finally *zuhūrat* (perfection of the old).

Similarly, in his architectural treatise Sinan informs the reader that Ottoman rebirth has links to the past. His confession about learning from ancient ruins to create works of *azim* (magnificence) with *nezāket* (elegance) and *cemile* (beauty) that finally *a'zam* (surpass) the past clearly resonates with Vasari's notions of rebirth. Sinan's dialogue with the Roman/Byzantine Hagia Sophia aligns Ottoman art with the West by using it as a model (*nūmūne*) for his works. Sinan acknowledges that through cultural appropriation his works are a result of learning, experimenting and restoring the old (*tecdid*) to finally create distinctly Ottoman masterpieces like the Süleymaniye and Selimiye that are 'worthy of the admiration of the humankind'.[139] Furthermore, his restoration of ancient buildings like the Ka'ba in Mecca mediates Ottoman rebirth with the classical Islamic past, signifying a more meaningful and specifically Ottoman definition of Renaissance. By uniquely looking at these Ottoman voices in the global Renaissance narrative, this work then fills a yawning gap in the scholarship of early modern Ottoman studies.

Bibliography

Adler, F. 'Die Moscheen zu Constantinopel: Eine architektonische baugeschictliche Studie,' (The Mosques of Constantinople: An Architectural Study), *Deutsche Bauzeitung* 8 (1874): 65–99.

Ali, Mustafa. *Epic Deeds of Artists: A Critical Edition of the Earliest Ottoman Text about the Calligraphers and Painters of the Islamic World.* Edited, translated and commented by Esra Akın-Kıvanç. Leiden: Brill, 2011.

Atasoy, N. and Julian Raby. *Iznik: The Pottery of Ottoman Turkey*. Edited by Yanni Petsopoulos, 14-49. London: Thames and Hudson, 1989.

Atıl, Esin. 'Ottoman Miniature Painting Under Sultan Mehmed II.' *Ars Oreintalis V*, IX (1973): 103-120.

Atıl, Esin. *Süleymanname: The Illustrated History of Süleyman the Magnificent*. Washington: National Gallery of Art, 1986.

Esin Atıl, 'The Image of Süleyman in Ottoman Art.' In *Süleyman the Second and His Time*. Edited by Halil Inalcik and Cemal Kafadar, 333-341. Istanbul: The Isis Press.

Babinger, F. 'Die türkische Renaissance: Bemerkungen zum Schaffen des grossen türkischen Baumeisters Sinân.' *Beiträge zur Kenntnis des Orients* 9 (1914): 67–88.

Baron, Hans. *The Crisis of the Early Italian Renaissance.* Princeton: Princeton University Press, 1966.

Beuchat, Robin. 'Échange interculturel et transfert de representations Sur les portraits turcs de Paolo Giovio', ('Intercultural exchange and transfer of representations of Turkish portraits of Paolo Giovio'), Université de Genève,' Arborescences: revue d'études françaises, n° 2, 2012, 6-7. Accessed August 23, 2014. http://www.erudit.org/apropos/utilisation.html.

Başbakanlık Arşivi, Muhimme Defteri 22, no. 171, Istanbul.

Başbakanlık Arşivi, Muhimme Defteri 10, no. 391, 253, 19B, 979, Istanbul.

Besnier- Kılıçioğlu, S. 'Sinan and Palladio: The Parallel Development of Two Master-Builders.' *The UNESCO Courier: a window opens on the world* XLI, no. 3 (1988). Accessed March 4, 2014. http://unesdoc.unesco.org/images/0007/000781/078126eo.pdf#77905.

Bhabha, H. *The Location of Cultures.* London & New York: Routledge, 1994. Kindle edition.

Bisaha, Nancy. *Creating East West: Renaissance Humanists and the Ottoman Turks.* Philadelphia: University of Pennsylvania Press, 2006.

Brotton, Jerry. *The Renaissance: A Very Short Introduction,* New York: Oxford University Press, 2006.

Brotton, J. *The Renaissance Bazaar: From the Silk Road to Michelangelo.* New York: Oxford University Press, 2002. Kindle edition.

Burckhardt, J. *The Civilisation of the Renaissance in Italy.* Pisa: Aonia edizioni, 2011.

Burioni, M. 'Vasari's Rinascita: History, Anthropology or Art Criticism.' Accessed January 29, 2016. https://www.academia.edu/2638258Vasari_s_rinascita._History_anthropology_or_art_criticis.

Castellano, D. J. 'The Renaissance Concept of Self as seen in Petrarch, Castiglione and Montaigne.' (Massachusetts: Boston University, 2002). Accessed May 23, 2016. http://www.arcaneknowledge.org/histschol/renaissance.htm

Coles, P. *Ottoman Impact on Europe*. Harcourt: Brace & World, 1968.

Denny, W. *Iznik: The Artistry of Ottoman Ceramics*. London: Thames and London, reprinted 2010.

Diez, Ernst. *Türk Sanatı: Başlangıcından Günümüze Kadar*. Translated by Oktay Aslanapa. Istanbul: Üniversite Matbaası, 1946.

Emerson, William and Robert L. Van Nice. 'Hagia Sophia and the First Minaret Erected After the Conquest of Constantinople.' *American Journal of Archaeology*, Vol. 54, No. 1 (Jan. - Mar., 1950): 33-34.

Ferguson, W. K. *The Renaissance in Historical Thought*. Cambridge, MA: Houghton Mifflin Company, 1948.

Fleischer, C. H. *Bureaucrat and Intellectual in the Ottoman Empire: The Historian Mustafa Ali, 1541-1600*. Princeton: Princeton University Press, 1986.

Gombrich, E. H. 'The Renaissance Conception of Artistic Progress and its Consequences.' In *Norm and Form: Studies in the Art of the Renaissance*, 1-10. London: Phaidon Press, 1966.

Goodwin, G. *A History of Ottoman Architecture*. London, UK: Thames and Hudson, 1971.

Grabar, Oleg. *The Formation of Islamic Art*. New Haven and London: Yale University Press, 1987.

Gurlitt, C. *Istanbul'un Mimari Sanatı, Architecture of Constantinople, Die Baukunst Konstantinopels*. Translated by Rezan Kæzæltan. Ankara: Enformasyon ve Dokumantasyon Hizmetleri Vakfı, 1999.

Hankins, J. 'Renaissance Crusaders: Humanist Crusade Literature in the Age of Mehmed II.' In *Dumbarton Oaks Papers,* Vol. 49, Symposium on Byzantium and the Italians, 13th-15th Centuries (1995): 111-207.

Hill, S. 'The Spectacle of the 'Other." In *Representation: Cultural Representations and Signifying Practices.* Edited by Stuart Hill. London: Sage Publications, 2003.

Howard, Deborah. *Venice and the East, The Impact of the Islamic World in Venetian Architecture 1100-1500.* New Haven and London: Yale University Press, 2000.

Hughes, A. 'Interpreting the Renaissance.' *Oxford Art Journal* 11 (1988): 77-78.

Inalcık, H. *The Ottoman Empire: The Classical Age 1300–1600.* London: Butler & Tanner, 1973.

Jardine, Lisa and Jerry Brotton. *Global Interest: Renaissance Art Between East and West.* London: Reaktion Books, 2000.

Jardine, Lisa. *Worldly Goods: A New History of the Renaissance.* London: W. W. Norton & Company, 1996.

Lehning, James R. *To be a Citizen: The Political Culture of the Early French Third Republic.* London: Cornell University Press, 2001.

Lewis, B. *Islam and the West.* London: Oxford University Press, 1993.

Libbrecht, Ulrich. 'Comparative Philosophy: A Methodological Approach.' In *Worldviews and Cultures: Philosophical Reflections from an Intercultural Perspective,* edited by Nicole Note et al., 31-68. Brussels: Springer, 2009.

Lowenthal, David. *The Past is a Foreign Country.* Cambridge: Cambridge University Press, 1985.

MacClean, Gerald. "Introduction: Re-Orienting the Renaissance." In *Re-Orienting the Renaissance,* edited by Gerald MacClean, 1-28. New York: Palgrave Macmillan, 2005.

Mack, Rosamond E. *Bazaar to Piazza: Islamic Trade and Italian Art, 1300-1600*. California: University of California, 2002.

Madison, D. Soyini. *Critical Ethnography: Method, Ethics, and Performance*. Los Angeles: Sage Publications, 2012.

Majer, Hans Georg. 'New Approaches in Portraiture.' In *The Sultan's Portrait: Picturing the House of Osman*, edited by Selmin Kangal, 336-375. Istanbul: İşBank, 2000.

McLaughlin, M. L. 'Humanist Concept of Renaissance and Middle Ages in the Tre- and Quattrocento.' *Renaissance Studies* 2 (1988): ix, 131-42.

Morkoç, Selen B. 'Reading Architecture from the text: The Ottoman Story of the Four Marble Columns.' Accessed February 9, 2018. https://www.academia.edu/27608699/Reading_Architecture_from_-Text_The_Story_of_the_Four_Marble_Columns

Murray, P. and L. Murray, *The Art of the Renaissance*. London, Thames and London, 1963.

Mustafa, M. *The Ottoman Renaissance: A Reconsideration of Early Modern Ottoman Art, 1413-1575*. New Jersey: Blue Dome Press, 2019.

Nagel, Alexander and Christopher Wood. 'Towards a New Model of Renaissance Anachronism.' *Art Bulletin* 87 (2005): 403-32.

Necipoğlu, Gülru. *The Age of Sinan: Architectural Culture in the Ottoman Empire*. London: Reaktion Books, 2005.

Necipoğlu, Gülru. 'From Byzantine Constantinople to Ottoman Konstantiniyye: Creation of a Cosmopolitan Capital and Visual Culture Under Sultan Mehmed II.' In *From Byzantium to Istanbul: 8000 Years of Capital*, edited by Nazan Ölçer, 265-276. Istanbul: Sabanci University, Sakip Sabanci Museum, 2010.

Necipoğlu-Kafadar, Gülru. *Muqarnas*, Vol. 3 (1985): 92-117. Accessed 8 February 8, 2018. http://www.jstor.org/stable/1523086?origin=JSTOR-pdf.

Necipoğlu, Gülru. 'The Serial Portraits of Ottoman Sultans in Comparative Perspective.' In *The Sultan's Portrait: Picturing the House of Osman,* edited by Selmin Kangal and translated by Priscilla Mary Işın. Istanbul: İşBank, 2000.

Nicomachean Ethics of Aristotle,' Book IV. http://www.sacred-texts.-com/cla/ari/nico/nico036.htm

Norton, C. 'Blurring the Boundaries: Intellectual and Cultural Interactions between Eastern and Western: Christian and Muslim Worlds.' In *The Renaissance and the Ottoman World.* Edited by Anna Contadini and Claire Norton. England: Ashgate Publishing Limited, 2013.

Panofsky, E. *Renaissance and Renascences in Western Art.* Almqvist & Wiksell, 1969.

Refik, Ahmet. *On Altıncı,* 8 (1935): 22-24.

Rogers, J. M. and R. M. Ward. *Süleyman the Magnificent.* London: British Museum Publications, 1990.

Ruggiero, Guido, ed. *A Companion to the Worlds of the Renaissance.* Malden: MA: Blackwell Publishing, 2007.

Rüsen, Jörn. "What is Historical Consciousness? - A Theoretical Approach to Empirical Evidence." Translated by Wolfgang Gebhard. Paper presented at Canadian Historical Consciousness in an International Context: Theoretical Frameworks, University of British Columbia, Vancouver, BC, 2001.

Sa'i, Mustafa. *Sinan's Autobiographies: Five Sixteenth Century Texts, Introductory Notes, Critical Editions, and Translations by Howard Crane and Esra Akın,* ed. Gülru Necipoğlu. Leiden: Brill, 2006.

Said, E. *Orientalism.* London: Penguin Books, 1995.

Sanstead, Lee. 'The Meaning of Michelangelo's David (5 September 2004).' Accessed February 19, 2017. http://www.sandstead.com/essays/david.html

Sardar, Z. *Orientalism*. Buckingham: Open University Press, 1999.

Selaniki, Mustafa Efendi. *Tarih-i Selaniki*. Edited by Mehmet Ipsirli. 2 vols. Istanbul: Türk Tarih Kurum Basımevi, 1989.

Vasari, Giorgio. *Le vite de' piu eccellenti architetti pittori, et scultori italiani da Cimabue insino a'tempi nostri*. Firenze: Torentino, 1550. http://bepi1949.altervista.org/vasari/vasari10.htm

Vasari, Giorgio. *Vasari's Lives of the Artists*. Translated by Jonathan Foster. New York: Dover Publications, 2005. Kindle edition.

Vasari, Giorgio. Preface to *The Lives of the Painters, Sculptors and Architects*. Accessed May 5, 2016. http://members.efn.org/~acd/vite/VasariPreface.html

Vasari, Giorgio. *The Lives of the Painters, Sculptors and Architects*. Accessed March 27, 2016. https://ebooks.adelaide.edu.au/v/vasari/giorgio/lives/part2.12.html

Vasari, Giorgio. PART 1 of *The Lives of the Painters, Sculptors and Architects*. Accessed May 5, 2016. http://members.efn.org/~acd/vite/VasariGioPisano.htm1

Vasari, Giorgio. Preface to Part II, *The Lives of the Painters, Sculptors and Architects*. Accessed May 5, 2016. http://members.efn.org/~acd/vite/VasariPreface2.html

Vasari, Giorgio. PART III of *The Lives of the Painters, Sculptors and Architects*. Accessed May 5, 2016. http://members.efn.org/~acd/vite/VasariMichelangelo7.html

Vasari, Giorgio. PART III of *The Lives of the Painters, Sculptors and Architects*. Accessed May, 5, 2016. http://members.efn.org/~acd/vite/VasariMichelangelo3.html

Vasari, Giorgio. PART III of *The Lives of the Painters, Sculptors and Architects*. Accessed May 5, 2016. http://members.efn.org/~acd/vite/VasariLeo.html

Yeni Cep Lügat. Istanbul: Envar Neşriyat, 2000.

Yerasimos, S. *Constantinople: Istanbul's Historical Heritage*. Paris: H. F. Ullmann Publishing, 2012.

The Mediterranean Renaissance: A Shared Heritage

ESSAY II

INTRODUCTION

What sense does it make to discuss the Renaissance solely as Italian, or Western-European phenomenon when we know that the Ottoman and Italian architects were influenced by each other's designs and techniques ... rulers in the East and West employed the same vocabulary and iconography of sovereignty and political legitimisation, engaged in the same practices and ceremonies designed to promote their power, read the same books, commissioned the same maps, and exchanged military, scientific and philosophical knowledge?[1]

The same spirit of classical Greece and Rome, which Italy, during the Renaissance rediscovered, also inspired the Ottomans from the former seat of the Eastern Roman Empire, Constantinople, to revive and give rebirth to their unique civilisation. The sultans as the inheritors of the Roman heritage referred to themselves as 'caesar' in official documents. Süleyman the Magnificent called himself the "Majestic Caesar", "Lord of the East and West" as did his great grandfather conqueror of Constantinople, Mehmed II (d. 1481).[2] The spirit of the age produced talented artists, architects and learned individuals who looked to the classical past for inspiration including Sinan and Michelangelo among other greats. This meant, the Renaissance was not a pan-European movement, but one of a shared legacy of the classical past experienced on both sides of the Mediterranean where Eastern and Western aesthetics often merged and influenced the aesthetic development of the age.

Historically speaking, the Ottoman Empire was founded at the beginning of the 14th century (c.1299-1300), which coincided with the beginning of the Renaissance movement in the city-states of Italy.[3] This historical parallelism would have, ultimately—through trade, diplomacy and conflict—seen a merging of the two cultures and their artistic development, and create a shared cultural heritage during the Renaissance (c. 1400-1600). Indeed, during the 15th and 16th centuries, the Ottoman Empire under Mehmed II (d.1481) and Süleyman the Magnificent (d. 1566) culminated in the centrifugal expansion of its visual and material cultural heritage throughout Europe.[4] Indeed, the impact of Ottoman cultural impressions went beyond Italy to eventually cover the entire continent. The convergence of these diverse early modern civilisations underscores the shared heritage of the Mediterranean Renaissance.

Historiography

Unfortunately, Western historiography concerning the Ottomans is still somewhat ambivalent and, despite the fact that such scholarly work is being produced, there remain scholars and academics that are constrained by the pan-European Renaissance legacy. In her 2004 work, *Creating East and West: Renaissance Humanists and the Ottoman Turks*, in a chapter entitled, *Epilogue: The Renaissance Legacy*, Bisaha acknowledges that Western views are still influenced by renaissance humanist responses to the Ottoman Turks.[5] Despite the fact that Renaissance humanists cultivated a further understanding of Muslim culture and religion, however erroneous, they also fostered the "hostile take on the Ottoman Turks", which "only served to nurture incipient ideas of Western superiority to Eastern rivals."[6] And therefore, the cultural expressions of the Ottomans were simply overlooked or neglected, and not taken very seriously.

Indeed, the notion of an Ottoman Renaissance has been suggested before. Late nineteenth and early twentieth-century architectural historians acknowledged the notion of an Ottoman Renaissance in the fifteenth and sixteenth centuries. As early as 1874, German architect Friedrich Adler acknowledged the 'spatial unity' and 'purist character' of Ottoman architecture.[7] As early as 1907 the idea of a Turkish Renaissance emerged, initiated by the German art historian and architect Cornelius Gurlitt, who recognised the originality of Ottoman architecture and the creative genius of Sinan and placed both within the Renaissance paradigm.[8] Gurlitt in fact dismissed the common idea that Ottoman architecture was a mere imitation of the Hagia Sophia and recognised instead that it was a product of a shared Mediterranean legacy:

> We have been enthusiastic in our praise of Italy, a country that at the end of the fifteenth century resurrected the art of ancient Rome after this achievement had lain dormant for over a thousand years. During the same period, however, buildings were erected on the Bosphorus that have been belittled for the simple reason that they were replicas of Hagia Sophia. Yet it is no less a renaissance of astounding individuality that sprang up from the soil made fertile by the spirit of ancient Greece. The revival of ancient perceptions of shape and form occurred here with the same freedom, independence, and boldness, with the same artistic and creative force, that was shaping the culture on the opposite shores of the Adriatic Sea.[9]

Gurlitt argues that the sharing and fusing of cultural values shaped the sixteenth century cultural revivalism of the Mediterranean basin of which the Ottomans were also significant participants. The uniqueness of Gurlitt's early view of Ottoman art has only been taken up recently.

Building on the work of Cornelius Gurlitt, in 1914 the German orientalist Franz Babinger, in an article titled "Die türkische Renaissance" (The Turkish Renaissance), compared Sinan's central plan domed mosques to the works of Bramante, Giuliano da Sangallo, Baldassare Peruzzi, and Michelangelo Buonarotti.[10] A year later Babinger even gave Sinan the sobriquet 'the Ottoman Michelangelo'.[11] The aim of his two articles was merely to invite historians and art historians to collaborate in bringing Sinan's works to universal recognition. His invitation was therefore like Necipoglu's call for a "fresh narrative". Babinger recognised that Sinan's imperial architectural monuments and also the aesthetic decorative styles of Ottoman fine arts were products sparked by the same Renaissance spirit of curiosity and competitiveness that exemplified the period elsewhere in Europe.

By 1925 Glück, in collaboration with Ernest Diez, produced *Die Kunst des Islam* which further elaborated the theory of the Turkish Renaissance. Diez later argued that the Ottoman dynasty needed monumental 'architectural representation' like the Romans.[12] He went on to emphasise the cross-cultural heritage of Ottoman and Italian Renaissance architecture in the Roman imperial tradition and attributed their similarities to a "period style". He called this style, "*Zeitstil*".[13] Turkish historian Halil Inalcık who in 1973 published *The Ottoman Empire: The Classical Age 1300–1600* reached the same conclusion; that is, that the Ottoman imperial state architecture is not authentically Turkish but rather a product of past and present exemplars from Roman/Byzantine, Islamic, and Timurid-Persianate-Turkic traditions from Central Asia.[14] Furthermore, in 1986 art historian Esin Atıl concurred with the view that, like its architecture, Ottoman art of the fifteenth and sixteenth centuries "saw the synthesis of European, Islamic and Turkish traditions and the creation of an artistic vocabulary that was unique to the Ottoman world."[15] The result of a shared heritage by the Ottomans produced unique art mediums from the monumental religious to secular works of art including tiles, calligraphy, illustrated manuscripts, ceramics, carpets, and embroidered textiles.[16] Combined with its ceremonials and pageants they reflected the power of the visual tastes of the sultan's court.[17]

Orientalism

The birth of orientalist literature and its impact on travellers to the Ottoman Empire and the Orient, from the 16th century onwards, was another factor that led to the demonising of the Ottoman 'Other' and stunted the West's reception of Ottoman art. However, according to Edward Said, any European interest that did exist for Islam and the Ottomans was not a result of natural curiosity but rather based in fear about 'threats' that were posed by the Muslim 'Other'.[18] Paradoxically, some Europeans actually admired this aspect of the Ottomans, but this had little impact on the historiography since then. While some visitors to the Ottoman Empire published accounts of their voyages, and descriptions of the lands of the 'Other', according to Ziauddin Sardar their tales "about Orientalism" contained nothing that was "neutral or objective"—Sardar believes that "[b]y definition it is a partial and partisan subject."[19] Ironically, even though the 'ism' in Orientalism is an artificial construct, the West has—for centuries—used it to define the cultural expression and identities of the 'Other'. Just as the Crusades would have been unthinkable without Islam, so too would Orientalism, without the Ottoman Turks. Sardar states that the "Orient which was closest to Europe acquired the character that eventually marked all the other Orients."[20] Claire Norton equally asserts, "As such the Ottoman Empire is figured as a quintessential Islamic, oriental, or Asian empire, where such terms carry the frequently pejorative connotations common in orientalist discourse."[21] For the Orientalist, therefore, Ottoman social and cultural expressions became the model on which Oriental despotism was constructed.

The Orient, therefore, was a framework created by Europeans, which enabled them to view themselves as superior over the 'Other'. This polarisation and 'us and them' mentality continue to this day, and modulates the marginalisation of Ottoman cultural expression. The critical distance established by postcolonial discourse, like that of Said's *Orientalism*, becomes problematic, as it is unlikely that foreign cultures can ever be presented objectively through language, power and appropriation.[22]

. . .

Revisionist Perspective: A Shared Heritage

Luxury objects and their exchange certainly became part and parcel of elite and merchant life of both East and West. Both cultures depended on such exchange. In fact, trade was the life-blood of not only European life but of Mediterranean life more generally in the global Renaissance. It is this cultural coexistence that provided the fluidity of the Renaissance age and which demands a broader Renaissance purview. Such artistic and cultural exchanges—through diplomatic, commercial, and of course, military means—gave the Ottomans from the fifteenth century onwards the opportunities to be influenced not just by the legacy of the West but also by the classical heritage of the Islamic East. The impact of such exchanges influenced the visual expressions of its court culture beyond its borders in Eastern and Western Europe. Thus, the broader understanding of the Renaissance goes beyond the parameters of the Mediterranean and seeks to find a holistic explanation of the Ottoman Renaissance in the Ottoman's own meaningful context. Although important, the Ottoman Renaissance does not stop at the revival of ancient Greek and Roman ideals, or its interaction with the West. In response to an obvious lacuna in the literature, this study explores the cultural, political and religious ties to the Ottomans' Eastern predecessors as well to demonstrate a larger context for the early modern Renaissance. Such an approach undermines the notion of Italian *rinascita* and nineteenth-century Eurocentric perceptions of the age.

According to David Abulafia, in *The Great Sea*, the diversity of the Mediterranean peoples, cultures and shared histories, can be represented by the figure of a merchant—one who carries food, words, ideas, religions and plagues across the water; bridging gaps between cultures and worlds.[23] The 'merchant' archetype, of course, would have also traded in luxury goods, such as carpets and ceramics, from Ottoman lands. For Norton it makes no sense to discuss the Renaissance solely as an Italian or European phenomenon especially, "when we know that Ottoman and Italian architects were influenced by each other's designs and techniques; artists crossed borders and worked for different patrons; rulers in the East and West employed the same vocabulary and iconography of sovereignty and political legitimisation, engaged in the same practices and ceremonies designed to promote their own power."[24] And therefore, due to cross-cultural interaction such as these, to consider a 16th century Europe, without also including the Ottomans, makes no sense.

The notion of a shared heritage in the Mediterranean is not a new idea, and was proposed as early as 1949, by Fernand Braudel, in *The Mediterranean and the Mediterranean World in the Age of Philip II.*[25] Italian traders had access to Egyptian goods both before and after the Ottoman expansion. When Vasco de Gama rounded the Cape of Good Hope in 1497, he did not do it as a result of Ottomans closing off the Orient to European trade, but to compete with Venice. When the old spice route Syria, Egypt, the Red Sea and the Persian Gulf came under the control of the Topkapı Palace in Istanbul in 1517 and consolidated this control in the Persian Gulf by 1534. Venice, through its commercial agreements with the Ottoman Empire continued to have trading access through these areas.[26] Thus, the Ottomans did not restrict the Mediterranean trade. As Braudel states:

> What is quite clear is that the Mediterranean had captured large portion of the pepper trade...trade with the Levant was flourishing...from the Persian Gulf ... to Red Sea...[27]

Braudel clearly points out, after 1550 "the difficult gateway to the Red Sea stood wide open, and a huge volume of trade flowed through."[28]

The making of the Renaissance cannot be fully understood without the Ottomans. Paul Coles (1968) in *The Ottoman Impact on Europe* argued, "[…] the development of Europe cannot be fully understood without a knowledge of the era of Turkish power."[29] Coles also noted, "[…] while the Ottoman empire suffered from growing administrative problems, the states of western and central Europe gradually increased their commercial and military resources."[30] Thus, the exchange of goods became a significant part of international negotiations during the 16th century Renaissance, and Ottoman contributions and involvement contributed to its making. Therefore, it would not be an overstatement to suggest that it would be impossible to come across a culture or civilisation that had managed to survive without encountering, knowing, exchanging goods and ideas, and even warring, with another. The attempt to focus on the domains where the Ottoman Empire and Europe came together to learn about, discover, and trade with, one another in times of peace—rather than times of confrontation or war—opens up new avenues for discovery. It also highlights the impact of cultural and artistic impressions that each region had on the other, which created 'fluidity' during the Renaissance—one that challenges the theory of European exclusivity during the period.

Revisionist historiography is more open to ideas of inclusive and global approaches to Renaissance studies and argues against the orientalist and elitist approaches to the period. In *Global Interest: Renaissance Art Between East and West,* Lisa Jardine and Jerry Brotton disagree with Edward Said's problematic theory of orientalism—they write, "such arguments enable us to circumvent an account of the marginalized, exoticized, dangerous East within the Renaissance studies as not only politically unhelpful but also historically inaccurate."[31] In other words, Said's *Orientalism* problematised the cultural binaries, of shared political and economic transactions, between East and West.[32] According to Jardine and Brotton, a step towards dissolving boundaries and creating a more receptive acknowledgment of the art of other cultures will begin when the 'Renaissance Man'— as "[...] constructed by Burckhardt and Freud"—is "dismantled".[33] Once this has been achieved, it will negate beliefs in "the antithetical, dark, dirty, exotic, Eastern Other as the negative to which that humane individualism has been opposed – the other ostensibly held at bay by its constructed version of civilization."[34] This highlights that not only was the 'Renaissance Man' a construct of 19th century ideology, but so too was the alien 'Other'.[35] According to Gerald MacClean:

> If the nineteenth century needed to historicise the artistic achievements of fourteenth- and fifteenth-century Italy by declaring them

> to signal a rebirth of European magnificence and civilisation, it also needed to ignore the great civilising achievements of the Ottomans by viewing that empire as it were a latter-day version of Rome, doomed to decay and fall.[36]

By bringing the Ottomans into the Renaissance narrative, the discourse also opens up other alternatives for future scholarship; where the art history of the Mediterranean civilisations of the 16th century were influenced through inter-cultural exchanges, in addition to being independently created. Similarly, Jardine also explores the Renaissance in her work, *Worldly Goods: A New History of the Renaissance*. In it she explores the material culture of 'the Age', when Renaissance culture in Italy stretched from its western borders, in Christendom, to the eastern reaches of the Islamic Ottoman Empire, "bringing this opulent epoch to life in all its material splendor and competitive acquisitiveness."[37]

Likewise, Deborah Howard, in *Venice and the East, The Impact of the Islamic World in Venetian Architecture 1100-1500*, focuses on the Venetian sense of identity in order to demonstrate whether they perceived themselves to be European (as opposed to the Ottoman 'Other')[38]. Howard's argument rests on the idea that Venetians ventured into Islamic territories, but with the identity of Westerners. For Howard, this affiliation with the Western world led to a feeling of "dislocation" as travellers that were compensated with "material gain, visual excitement and devotional experiences."[39] Her efforts, to illustrate how Venetian narratives appropriated Islamic elements, stress the impact that the former had on the latter, and add weight and attention to the Renaissance debate. Additionally, Howard achieves this without looking at the argument in reverse. Instead, she addresses broader issues that arose from the cultural interactions, and this, avoids placing blame on previous eras. Reconciliatory efforts, such as Howard's, to dissolve boundaries can only improve the art history debate, and move the discourse toward a more objective analysis of the art of the 'Other'. Therefore, just as the Renaissance Man and Ottoman Other were constructs of 19th century ideology, art history as it exists in the twenty-first century will become an all-inclusive discourse—a new construct where only art triumphs, and an avenue by which to dissolve cultural boundaries, irrespective of any 'isms'.

Recent work by Rosamond Mack, *Bazaar to Piazza: Islamic Trade and Italian Art, 1300-1600*, is part of a growing body of scholarly work that focuses on the artistic exchanges that occurred during the Renaissance in the Mediterranean basin, through trade in non-figurative goods (e.g., carpets, ceramics and silks). Whilst existing work already suggests that artistic exchange occurred in the medieval period, Mack extends the discourse by asserting that these artistic exchanges also occurred in Renaissance Italy. In doing so, Mack challenges the traditional view that Renaissance artistic achievements were a self-contained phenomenon. Instead, she believes that European aesthetics and tastes lie at the core of views held by traditional Renaissance art historians. In fact, the European reliance on luxury goods led to the growth of elite and merchant classes whose existence depended on cross-cultural dialogues between the binaries. Thus, in Italy, there emerged a hybrid form of artistic production but Mack does not view this as having hindered the cultural blossoming of either Renaissance or Ottoman cultures. In fact, Mack concludes her book by writing, "[s]ixteenth century East-West trade and artistic exchange softened a clash of civilizations, establishing a historical precedent for cultural coexistence and mutual enrichment."[40] It is this mutual, cultural coexistence that provided the fluidity of the Renaissance Age, whereby artistic and cultural exchanges—through diplomatic, commercial, and of course, military means—gave the Ottomans of the Süleymanic era the opportunities to contribute to, and become intertwined in, the Renaissance narrative. It should also be noted that their contributions extended beyond Italy, to areas within Northern and Eastern Europe, including England, the Netherlands, Poland and Muscovy.

Other academics pose more pointed questions about whether the Renaissance in Italy, and subsequently Northern Europe, deserve exclusive status. Jack Goody, for example, scrutinises the Italian model in relation to other parallel 'renaissances' that *may* [emphasis added] have taken in other cultural areas, that is, mainly from Islamic societies and China. As a social anthropologist, Goody does not believe that modernity and capitalism began with the Italian Renaissance.[41] Instead, he claims that "teleologically inclined Europeans" invented this view.[42] More specifically, Goody writes:

> Where Europe deferred [...] was that to make such a burst forward, in the subject of artistic works for example, the culture had to partially free itself from the restrictions imposed by a hegemonic, monotheistic religion, namely Christianity, and to open up to the wider world of classical, 'pagan' or polytheistic Greece and Rome.[43]

As Goody suggests this revolution could not have happened without non-European influences.[44] Acknowledging that trade with the Ottoman Empire "[...] was a prominent part of the economic revival of Europe," the historian ironically who believes in parallel renaissances, fails to recognise that it was through such economic activity between East and West that contributed to inter-cultural exchanges.[45] While recognising the golden age of medieval Islam in Chapter 4 of his book, "Rebirth of Islam", he remains ambivalent in his concluding remarks, instead, questioning whether there was a Turkish 'renascence', thus leaving the discussion in disarray.[46]

Renaissance Convergence

There is no denying that the close connections formed through trade, and intellectual and cultural influences during the medieval period, between Christendom and Islam, shaped the course of the Renaissance. The degree of traffic between these two civilisations, which shared the same Abrahamic tradition, reinforces the 'many renaissances' theory. It also subverts the idea that cultural rebirth was a phenomenon exclusively linked to the city-states of Italy, between 1300 and 1550.[47] In fact, there were many cross-interactions between East and West, including:

- mutual influences on design and aesthetic practice;[48]
- the movement of wealth and trade within the Mediterranean basin;[49]
- a growing European taste for Eastern spices, coffee, textiles and carpets;[50]
- the Ottoman need for English tin and metal (to make canons);[51]
- Sultan Mehmed II's taste for Italian medals, classical Greek histories—such as the *Illiad*—and having his portrait painted by Italian Renaissance masters like Gentile Bellini and Costanzo de Ferrara;[52]
- Süleyman the Magnificent's taste for "Florentine sculpture"[53], and
- the exchange of maps and navigation knowledge.[54]

Additionally, large numbers of merchants from Venice, France and—by the latter quarter of the 16th century—England and the Netherlands, conducted trade in Istanbul, Damascus, Cairo and Budapest, which contributed to a period that was more inclusive than exclusive of other cultures. Consequently, the growing inter-cultural exchange of ideas that new trade routes created made the Renaissance more fluid than it had previously been. Through these exchanges, both sides could observe the other, but more importantly—as Dalrymple states—"[a]t all levels, the Ottoman world impinged directly on Renaissance life."[55] Had it not been for the flow of goods between East and West, and from West to East, the achievements that are typically associated with the Renaissance would not have occurred. It is this cultural connection, combined with the intellectual awakening that came to represent the Renaissance, which clearly demonstrates the interplay between cultures from the eastern and western sides of the Mediterranean, and is just as significant as any process of self-regeneration that drew from Greek, Roman or Islamic roots. As Jack Goody states, "[a] renascence or reformation such as was experienced in Europe [...] is in principle possible in any literate society."[56]

. . .

Representations of a Renaissance City

For the Ottomans—looking back on their medieval Islamic and Central Turkic heritage, and from the onset of the conquest of Constantinople in 1453—they very likely saw themselves as heirs to classical Rome. In fact, they began to represent this aspiration by incorporating the past into their art and architecture, and therefore, "[…] the past may be understood as a part of their symbolic control of the land and as an attempt to position themselves within the larger context of world history as the rightful heirs of the Roman/Byzantine Empire."[57] They also began to see themselves as part of the once glorious city, Constantinople, and represent the new Ottoman Istanbul in religious and secular works just as their Renaissance counterparts in Venice. For example, in certain miniature paintings art historians have identified both a glorification of Constantinople/Istanbul and its transformation from a Christian to Islamic city. Additionally, the Ottomans also took pride in their architectural achievements; from mosques to bazaars, aqueducts, bathhouses and fountains. This can be seen in the works of Matrakçi Nasuh (1480-c.1564), one of Süleyman's chief artists, who arrived to Süleyman's palace from Bosnia, and trained under the *devshirme* system where Christian boys from the conquered territories of the Balkans were taken from their families, brought to the Topkapı Palace, converted to Islam and educated under the Ottoman education system. Those who showed skill and merit rose to positions of high office. As a miniaturist, calligrapher and painter, he produced illustrated books that featured townscapes from Toulon in France, to Baghdad. Nasuh also joined Süleyman on expeditions against the Safavids, between 1533 and 1536, and in his *Bayan-i Manazil-i Safar-i Iraqayn-i Sultan Süleyman Khan* he described and illustrated the cities he had visited; depicting roads that connected cities such as Baghdad and Istanbul, as well as the cities themselves. In one of his famous paintings *Map of Istanbul* that resemble a topographic map he was able to depict a bird's eye view of Istanbul, including all its public structures, in remarkable detail providing the impression of civic pride of this Ottoman city. In the centre of the painting, the Golden Horn runs vertically, separating the Galata section—with its famous tower—(on the left) from the city proper (on the right), which includes major structures such as Topkapı Palace, Hagia Sophia, At Meydanı (Roman / Byzantine Hippodrome), Grand Bazaar, Old Palace and the complex (*külliye*) of Mehmed II. In the 1530s, Nasuh's painting was an important document for the study of Istanbul, and the illustration is an example of the topographic genre of painting, which was initiated by Nasuh and continued for centuries *(Figures 1-2).*[58]

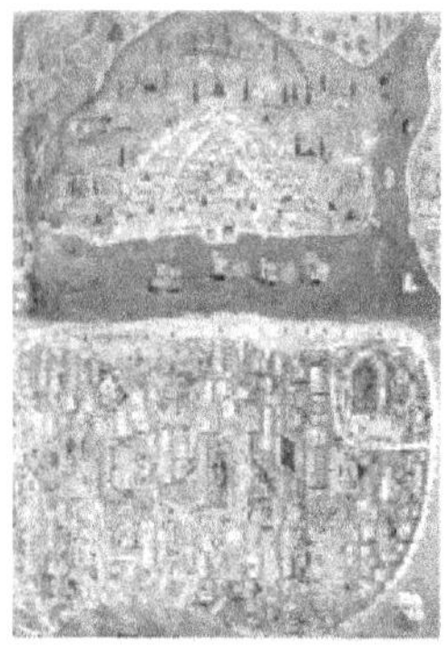

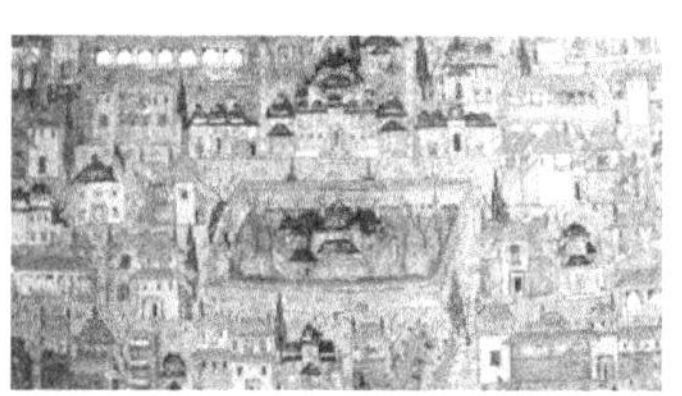

Figures 1, 2. Left, Matrakci Nasuh's map of Istanbul from Menazil- I Irakeyn; below, Matrakci Nasuh's map of the Hippodrome in Istanbul from Menazil- I Irakeyn. Photograph reproductions.

In another Nasuh painting, the artist's meticulous attention to detail and use of vibrant colours, such as red, orange and black, is quite striking. These two particular Nasuh paintings can be read in two ways. Firstly, they offer testimony to the makings of a Muslim city, as depicted by the central location of the Old Palace, and secondly, they portray the making of an Ottoman imperial capital. As Avcıoğlu states, "[...] if the appropriation of the city's center and the upper castle with fortified walls were the instruments for projection of the Ottoman power, together they assumed a kind of legitimizing quality."[59]

Therefore, in 1537, these two representations of the Ottoman capital by Nasuh—with its Old Palace and fortress of Topkapı— became the first aesthetic manifestations of the most characteristic shape of an Ottoman city. These early Ottoman miniature paintings are also imbued with a sense of the artist's pride, suggested by his use of vibrant colours that allude to a city that has been resurrected and, because of the Ottomans, is alive again. The 'life-giving force' that the artist depicts as having been bestowed on a once dilapidated city is like an act of gratitude to the Islamisation of the former Byzantine/Roman capital, and a means of symbolically securing a unified Islam. Additionally, the *Ottomanising* of the city should also be attributed to the architectural specificity of Topkapı Palace, the palace of Ibrahim Pasha, the Grand Bazaar and the bathhouses, where "[...] an emphasis on the archetypal topographic sign of Muslim authority was not in itself sufficient for the Ottoman imperial identity of the city."[60] The sprawling nature of the city, depicted in Nasuh's paintings, indicates a kind of public and communal interconnectedness signifying the fulfilment of Mehmed II's vision a century earlier where in his words on the foundation deed of the Fatih (Conqueror) Mosque, "True art is to create a glorious city. And to fill the people's hearts with felicity."[61]

The significance of the Nasuh paintings (introduced above) indicate diverging cultural preferences between the Roman, Byzantine and Ottoman Empires—as indicated by the Hippodrome, Hagia Sophia and the mosques. According to Edward Muir, painters in Renaissance Italy (like Lorenzetti in Siena) used similar images to represent their cities. Through the invention of in the 15th century of the bird's eye view of cities he "created the illusion of civic totality."[62] Additionally, these reflections—to visitors and local inhabitants alike—"[...] reflected [the] changing social and political conditions, modeled ideal arrangements of power, and created opportunities to subvert or redefine power relationships."[63] Certainly, while the Ottoman Empire was a centralised entity, its redefinitions of power relationships are also evident in paintings, such as Nasuh's. As for its architecture, the growing power of the grand vizier, Ibrahim Pasha, was displayed very in early during his reign in the form of his grandiose palace in the Hippodrome—where most of the city's 16th century royal weddings and circumcision ceremonies took place.

Civic processions intermingled with religious symbolism to define the city, and were integral features of early modern societies. In fact, civic processions were derived from ecclesiastical processions in Renaissance Italy, mainly in Venice clearly depicted in Bellini's 1496 painting *Procession of the True Cross in Piazza San Marco* and *Miracle of the Cross at the Bridge of S. Lorenzo* (1500). As Muir states, "[...] the doge, completely appropriated the liturgical rites of St Mark to create the most comprehensive state cult of any city-state in Italy."[64] After 1517, the Ottomans also—in accordance with their religious tradition—used their caliph status and the relics of the Prophet, which had been brought to the palace by Süleyman's father, Selim I, to further sanctify Süleyman's position. The palace and the city where the "[...] banner of the Prophet was paraded through the streets of Constantinople" was a constant reminder of the new order, and available for all to see.[65] These similar representations of Istanbul and Venice respectively, reinforce the notion that the Renaissance was not unique to the city-states of Italy, but also a movement that transcended cultural borders. As can be seen in the Ottoman example, the concept of looking back to the past and using it as the basis for creating a new society, and ways of living, was not unique to Renaissance Italy.[66]

Mehmed II: an Ottoman Renaissance Prince

Inter-cultural activities during the 15th and 16th centuries allowed the Ottoman court to pursue Italian Renaissance architects and artists, and commission them to work in Istanbul, and such initiatives led to the construction of buildings such as Topkapı Palace and the mosque of Mehmed II—displaying a hybrid of styles. Certainly, the fusion of architectural styles used in, for example, the palace of Süleyman's great grandfather, Mehmed II, cannot be ignored. The 1452 architectural treatise by Leon Batista Alberti stresses that the principal temple of a city should be planned in its centre, specifically, it should be isolated in the centre of an ample square and raised on a podium to elevate its dignity.[67] Similarly, Spiro Kostof has pointed out the immense complexity of Mehmed II's 'modernism':

> Nothing so early in the Western renaissance has this grandeur. We have to remember that Constantinople was originally created as the New Rome. In her the Conqueror inherited the one city that safeguarded the Classical tradition in the eastern half of the Christian world as authentically as Rome did in the West. After the fall of Constantinople, the Turks were well placed to stage their own renaissance.[68]

The opportunity for the Ottomans to "stage their own renaissance" was created during Süleyman's 46-year reign; the Süleymanic Age. This period represented a time that, according to Turkish art historian, Esin Atıl, "saw the synthesis of European, Islamic and Turkish traditions and the creation of an artistic vocabulary that was unique to the Ottoman world."[69] This era in Ottoman history embodied the:

> [...] age of giants among architects and artists. Some of the most famous were Sinan, the great architect; Nigari, the portraitist; Matrakci, the illustrator of histories; Sahkulu, the creator of the *saz* style, Kara Memi, the innovator of the naturalistic genre; Mehmed, the master bookbinder, and Karahisari, the celebrated calligrapher.[70]

Atıl believes that the influence of Western art—after it had been introduced to the Ottoman court—on the art of the Ottomans was due to Mehmed II's "westernization of the empire."[71] Additionally, due to his patronage of Italian artists, such as Bellini, this "westernization" contributed to the eventual "Turkification" of Ottoman art of the Süleymanic Age.[72]

Indeed, portraiture was also influenced by the likes of Bellini, and representations of human form—while not sculptural—were reproduced in three dimensional paintings, such as Bellini's portrait at the court of Mehmed II and miniature paintings by Ottoman artists, e.g., Sinan Bey, Ahmed of Bursa, Nigari, Matrakçi Nasuh, Nakkaş Osman and Lokman. The works of these Ottoman artists—particularly Sinan Bey, Ahmed of Bursa and Nigari[73]—who had been influenced and taught by the Venetian artists like Bellini and Costanzo de Ferraro from Mehmed II's court, came to produce a cross-hybridity of Ottoman artworks, such as Ahmed of Bursa's portrait, *Mehmed II Smelling a Rose* and Sinan Bey's three quarter profile of the sultan.[74]As Claire Norton states:

Sinan Bey's ability to translate Western and Eastern artistic vocabularies and traditions, together with his ability to speak Italian, meant that he was sent as a cultural ambassador to Venice at the same time that Bellini was performing a similar role in Istanbul.[75]

Additionally, Ottoman work by Nigari (portrait of Süleyman the Magnificent) circulating in Europe after 1574 influenced Italian artists, such as Paolo Giovio (1483-1552) and Pietro Bertelli (c.1599), as can be seen in their portraitures of Ottoman sultans in the Veronese series, which were later used as inspiration by Lokman and Nakkaş Osman in the latter part of the 16th century.[76] These inter-cultural exchanges highlight the nature of patron-client relationships in the world of Ottoman miniature paintings. Regardless of whether they depicted Ottoman dynastic leaders or more 'common' patrons, such as vizier Sokollu Mehmed Pasha, they are evidence of changing attitudes and imperial ideologies. Additionally, the overlapping Renaissance narratives signify that as well as a desire to be different and belong to a unique culture; there were also a desire to remain open to cultural borrowings. These cultural and artistic exchanges reinforce assertions, such as those of Brotton, that a "more global perspective on the nature of the Renaissance is needed where a series of Renaissances throughout the regions, each with their own highly specific and separate characteristics [...] overlapped and exchanged influences with the more classical and traditionally understood Renaissance centred on Italy."[77]

Sinan and Palladio: Architectural convergence

When looking at comparative developments in architecture, during the 16th century, it can be argued that no architects shaped the visual identities of their respective cities more than Sinan (c.1489-1588) and Palladio (1508-1580). Reinforcing Claire Norton's words above, the convergence of their styles, during this period, contribute to our discussion of parallel efflorescence and centre around the sixth century Roman/ Byzantine Hagia Sophia, which greatly inspired the architectural styles of both architects. However, despite their shared inspiration, the two architects—Sinan in the East and Palladio in the West—produced very different types of work, and in fact, the two never met. Sinan primarily designed religious buildings while Palladio built a series of villas in the Venetian region of Italy. Despite their differences, their basic similarity was their parallel development of architectural methods; "gradually parting company with their sources, building up a precise figurative lexicon and, above all searching for typologies and formal variants."[78] The various planometric combinations from their output can be reduced to a single spatial pattern that was square in shape, namely the "'nine spaces' of Palladio's villas, and the 'spatial unity created by a dome' of Sinan's mosques."[79] The two architects' adoption of this 'square' formula would undergo many changes during the course of the 16th century *(Figures 2a-c).*

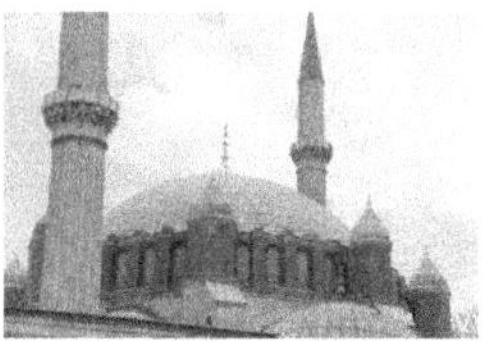

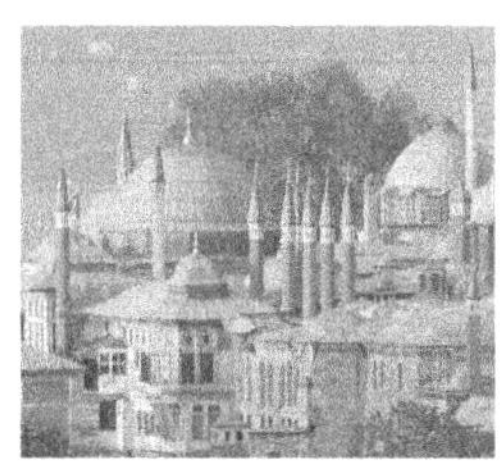

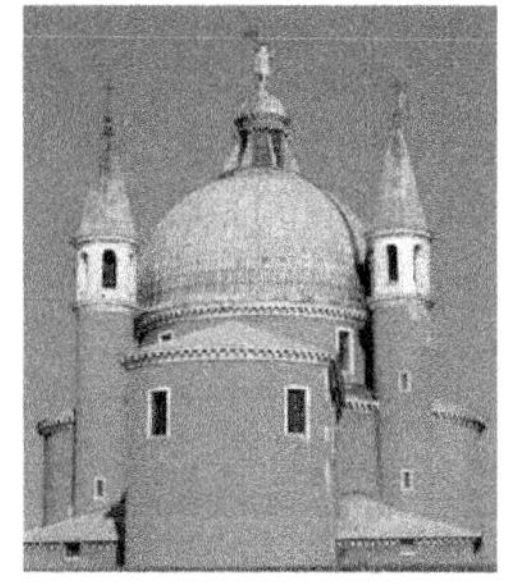

Figures 2a, 2b, 2c. Right, the central dome and slender minarets of Sinan's Selimiye Mosque in Edirne (1575); centre, domes and chimneys of the harem of the Topkapı Palace by Sinan (1579); below, back elevation of Il Redentore (1592) of Palladio, Venice, showing similarities with Sinan's work in Figures 2a and 2b. Photographs by Metin Mustafa, January, 2015 / 1999.

However, its formulation attests to their application of rigorous and critical conceptual methods. The art historian, Rudolf Wittkower, demonstrates in *Architectural Principles in the Age of Humanism* that all Palladian villas have a regular rectangular outline, that is, "nine-spaces" modified by two symmetrical wings, which determine the principles of spatial distribution.[80] For Sinan, however, in order to achieve his conceptual design of spatial unity, but on a very large scale (through the use of a dome, like Palladio's), led him to follow methods that were based on Mannerist experimentation. The fruits of such experimentation can be seen in examples, such as the Süleymaniye Mosque in Istanbul, and—Sinan's ultimate work, where he finally developed a solution for creating uninterrupted space under a single dome—the Selimiye Mosque in Edirne. As Yerasimos notes, "[i]t is interesting to observe how in a mind as creative as Sinan's an obsessive dialogue with a model can evolve into a path toward genuine originality."[81] Unfortunately, Sinan's mosque designs, which used a central dome flanked by two half-domes, has often misled art historians whose analysis have not taken account of his Mannerist style. According to Besnier-Kılıçoğlu, Sinan's "failure to recognize the continuous development of syntactical conceptual methodology leads them to see the Süleymaniye Mosque as a copy of the sixth-century Byzantine basilica of Hagia Sophia."[82]

There is no denying Sinan's impact on Ottoman artistic creativity. A reading of folio 190b in the 1582 illustrated manuscript *Surname-i Hümayun* suggests that Ottoman artists eventually ceased using Hagia Sophia—which had long dominated the discourse until the building of the Süleymaniye—for their architectural inspiration. Instead, they created their own original and creative masterpieces. The float of the Süleymaniye dominates the entire folio 190b signifying this shift in Ottoman architectural vision for the future architectural aesthetic. By this stage, Sinan's distinct architectural style had entered Ottoman art consciousness, and while 16th century writer, Mustafa Ali, in *Epic Deeds of Artists*, does not set any criteria by which one can define innovation and originality he stresses great emphasis on the concept of innovation as he tries to trace, and bring to the fore, the period and its individual styles. Ali enthusiastically writes about inventors, a group to which Sinan surely belonged, and describes their "pleasing styles" and "much-admired [stylistic] innovations," which he praised as being "impeccable", "inimitable" and "the most illustrious".[83]

The genius of Sinan is clearly demonstrated in his hundreds of complexes and buildings, most of which are still standing. However, it is rather sad to note that the architectural and aesthetic similarities between Sinan and his Renaissance contemporaries have either been dismissed, on culturally biased grounds, or simply overlooked.

However, in Palladio's Redentore Church and Sinan's Süleymaniye Mosque one can see an "insistence of both architects [...] on using the central hall and on applying symmetry on both sides bears a resemblance to the 9SG structure."[84] Furthermore, both Sinan and Palladio believed that beauty requires the complete agreement between all of a structure's design components, and for a comprehensive correspondence between the whole and its parts. Their search for 'beauty' is strongly associated with their structural, programmatic and mathematical order, and adherence to strict rules of composition.

While Palladio integrated the architectural history of his culture into his architectural style, as can be seen in the Palazzo Thiene—through his use of pilasters and the rusticated ornamentation of the early Renaissance Florentine style—as well as the high classical style he used in the Villa La Rotonda, and the baroque decoration that adorns the Palazzo Porto Breganze. Similarly, Sinan referred to decorative models that originated from his cultural heritage, which was rich with his region's traditions and Islamic symbiosis. Therefore, Sinan used many Turkish and Byzantine elements, and fused them to produce a distinctly Ottoman style. In an analysis of Sinan's work, Besnier-Kılıçcoğlu describes some of it as follows: "arched windows of Byzantine origin in the central domes to transfer downward the dynamic thrust essential to the support of such structures; ogee arch openings, showing Persian influence, in the walls of the main structure on order to emphasise the vertical composition."[85] However, as influenced as they were by their cultural heritage, they did not plagiarise earlier work. Rather, their innovative style and genius rest in having assimilated, and adapted, the constructive and ideological rationales that ran through their shared heritage, and embodied the Renaissance period in the Mediterranean basin.

Sinan and Michelangelo: Two Renaissance Masters

In order to gain a better understanding of Sinan's self-image it is pertinent to briefly compare his autobiographies with that of the Renaissance artists. Sinan's autobiographies are much shorter in length. According to Selen B. Morkoç, they are "in line with the Renaissance genre of 'vitae' such as that written by Condivi (d. 1574) for Michelangelo or by Manetti (d. 1497) for Brunelleschi.[86] Spiro Kostof views the works of Sinan as a renewal phase in the history of Ottoman art, one that is comparable to recent scholarly interest in Mediterranean antiquity in Renaissance Italy.[87] For many scholars including Kostof, Godfrey Goodwin and Doğan Kuban, interpreting the architectural past the Ottomans inherited after the conquest of Constantinople in 1453 began with Sinan in the 16th century. Sinan's dialogue with the past, the sixth century Eastern Roman / Byzantine Hagia Sophia is the expression of this interpretation process.[88] Sinan, in his autobiographies confirm this obsession with the Hagia Sophia.[89]

Like his Renaissance contemporaries, Sinan composed his treatise "… in order that a memorial and record [of his artworks] endure through the pages of time."[90] The treatise lists all his works—mosques, hospices, madrasas, bridges, palaces, fountains and countless other structures—as a testimony of the decades of learning and adapting of the old into something new in the creation of a distinct Ottoman style. Sinan acknowledges of having learnt from the ancient ruins and monuments he visited throughout his military career and journeys. Having learned from the ancient ruins around him by *tecdid* (restoring, renovating and renewing), he refined his *sūret, üsl'ub* (style) and gave rebirth to the old.[91] Sinan attained *'azim* (magnificence), *nezāket* (elegance, refinement), *cemile* (beauty) and *zuhūrat*, literally meaning perfection, through a rebirth of stylistic progression in his buildings leading to his distinct new *sūret* (style).[92] Like the Renaissance masters, Sinan saw a linear progress in his work. "Day by day many types of buildings being created, and refinement increased", he writes, signifying the progression of art through the ages and culminating in "art attain[ing] complete realization."[93] Praising his 1548 work of adapting the Hagia Sophia model with his style in the Şehzade Mosque in Istanbul, Sinan confirms, "such artistry had not been previously accomplished by any master" because previous works imitating the *Ayasōfya tarzı*[*nda*] (Hagia Sophia style) structure "did not possess elegance".[94] Sinan informs the reader that the Roman/Byzantine structure of the Ayasōfya *tarzı[nda]* became the inspiration for his works and that these works in return became a *nūmūne* (model) for the Süleymaniye Mosque (1557–8). In Spiro

Kostof's words the Ottomans were now in a position to "stage their own renaissance."[95]

Concurring with Kostof's line of argument of the links to classical antiquity in the Mediterranean, Necipoğlu also sees parallelisms in architectural aesthetics in Renaissance Italy and in the Ottoman Empire. Byzantine structures displayed an architectural heritage that ran parallel to that of Istanbul and Venice, and was perhaps made even more pronounced by their similar geographies tied to the Mediterranean Sea.[96] Oral and written accounts, as well as drawings by European diplomats and artists, became the media through which Ottoman architecture became more widely known. Michelangelo, for example, while known to have studied the domes of Florence Cathedral, and the Pantheon, he most likely included those of Hagia Sophia and Sinan's Süleymaniye mosque in Istanbul.[97] Similarly, Michelangelo who once contemplated entering the service of Sultan Bajezid II may have collected information about Sinan's mosques and his technology of dome construction—particularly considering that Süleymaniye mosque and St. Peter's Basilica were constructed at around the same period, i.e., between 1548-1557[98] and 1552-1564[99], respectively. In fact, when Pietro della Valle visited Istanbul in 1614, he noticed similarities between the two structures:

> [T]hat which is noteworthy are the mosques, in particular four or five of them built by the Turkish emperors, all of them situated on the highest hilltops in such a way that they almost form a row, visible from one end of the sea to the other and equally distributed along the whole length of the city. They are well built in marble and differ little in architecture from one another, being in the form of a temple composed of a domed square, like the design of St. Peter's in Rome by Michelangelo; and I believe they have taken as their model Hagia Sophia which they encountered there.[100]

Pietro della Valle also wrote that he had promised to bring back paintings of Sinan's mosques and the Hagia Sophia, so that Italian architects could use them as sources of inspiration.[101] When Michelangelo took over the project of St Peter's from his predecessors, Bramante and Sangallo, the interior had already been completed. While the original architects had proposed the use of a single-shell dome, Michelangelo's original design opted for spur-like buttresses with paired columns, which alternated with windows and included four smaller domes on each corner. Interestingly, Michelangelo had proposed something very similar to the Hagia Sophia and the mosques of Sinan.[102] While one cannot make any claims with absolute certainty, it is possible that Michelangelo's original design—with its stylistic resemblance to Sinan's mosques—may indicate that he found inspiration in the work of his Ottoman counterpart. However, after Michelangelo's death in 1564, the hemispherical dome that he intended for was modified to resemble the one belonging to Florence Cathedral.

By the middle of the 16th century, Sinan had codified the architectural style of the Ottoman mosque and this codification may explain why the influence of Italian architectural innovation began to wane in the East. However, his experimentation did not stop him from learning about Italian architecture, in particular, through his close friendship with the *dragoman* Yunus Bey, who was sent to Venice on diplomatic missions. Such was their friendship that Sinan also built a mosque, in Istanbul, in Bey's honour. It is likely that through connections such as Bey; through oral reports and architectural prints, Sinan would have learned of the construction of St. Peter's in Rome. As a side note, the plans for the build were once kept at the office of royal architects at Vefa, in Istanbul, but have since been lost. However, certain French embassy letters from the 18th century report of Sultan Mahmud I's chief architect having, at his disposal, a collection of prints and plans—including a Turkish translation of the treatise of architecture.[103] Francesco Dei Marchi also mentions Ottoman travellers who, during the 1540s, saw St. Peter's Basilica:

> [T]he temple of S. Pietro in Rome is the most magnificent in all of Christendom, and when it is built according to the design and model none other like it will be found anywhere [...] and certainly

> all men on earth desire that this temple should be completed and seek to aid and favor its completion, even including the Turks, enemies of the true faith. I spoke with some of them in Rome, who desired that this Church may be finished according to its beautiful and marvellous beginnings.[104]

Therefore, it is possible that Sinan also had access to Italian plans that were carried by returning Ottoman travellers. Additionally, Burns suggests that Antonio Salamanca's engravings of Sangallo's wooden model of St Peter's may have been available to Sinan, which could explain the more complex piers of the Süleymaniye mosque *(Figures 3, 4).*[105]

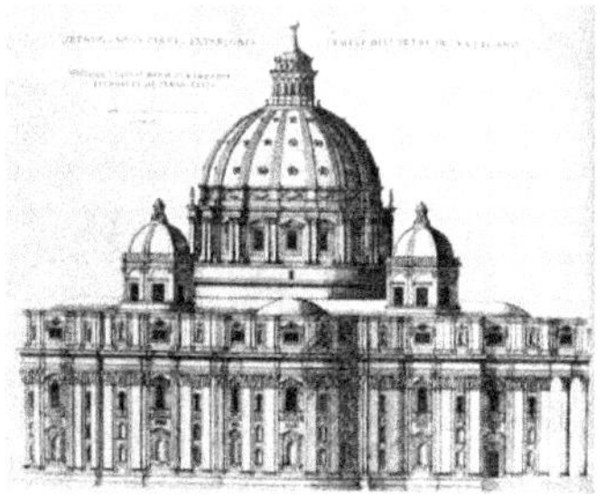

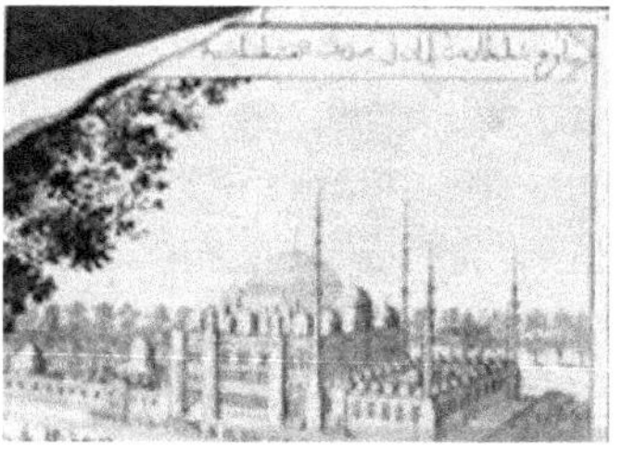

Figures 3, 4. Left, Michelangelo, elevation of the exterior of St. Peter's in an engraving by Antonio Salamanca, 1547; below, 18th century engraving of the Süleymaniye Mosque, Fischer von Erlach, 1721. Photograph reproductions.

While one can only speculate on Sinan's level of access to, and awareness of, designs for St. Peter's it is noteworthy that he decided to revise the façade of his masterpiece, the Selimiye mosque in Edirne (1569-75). By abandoning the mosque's pyramidal cascade of domes and introducing a lateral façade, in order to balance its horizontal tiers, the mosque became more similar to Michelangelo's church in Rome, and Alberti's Santa Maria Novella in Florence. The updated Selimiye façade, which reflects Renaissance aesthetics, demonstrates that the similarities on both sides of the Mediterranean may have been due to cross-cultural exchanges of idea —through oral and written reports, and architectural prints (*Figures 5, 6*).

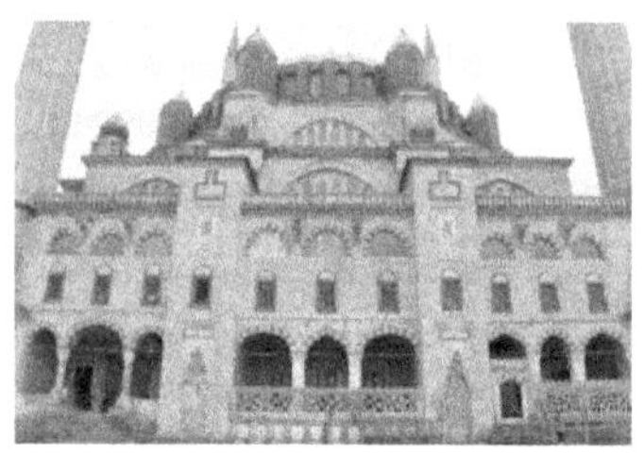

Figures 5, 6. Right, the geometric designs of the façade of the Selimiye (1575). Photograph by Metin Mustafa, December, 2014; below, façade of Santa Maria Novella completed by Alberti in 1470. Photograph by M. Aksoy, June, 2011.

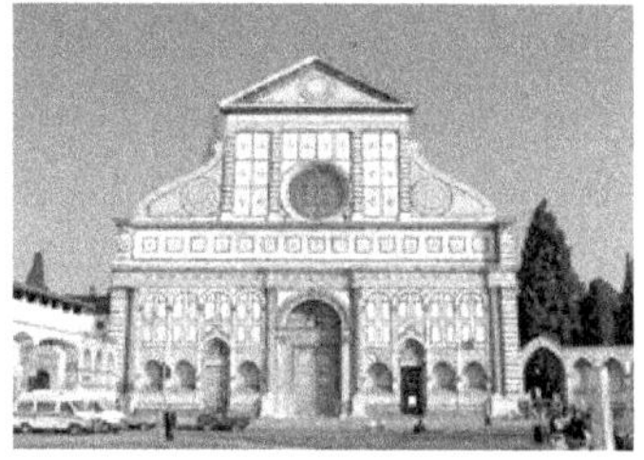

The relationship with classical antiquity in the early modern Mediterranean civilisations with Sinan's architecture is valuable in re-orienting our understanding of the Renaissance. This affinity represents the "relationships among world civilisations freed from the Western-Eastern stereotypes and hierarchies" and reinforces Necipoğlu's call for a "fresh narrative".[106]

Renaissance Humanism

Ottomans, unlike their Italian counterparts, were unlikely to have shared the opinions of Fontenelle, a 17th century French intellectual who stated, "[a] reading of the Ancients cleared the ignorance and the barbarity of preceding centuries [...] It suddenly gave us ideas of Truth and Beauty which would have taken a long time to reach."[107] However, an autobiographical passage written by the 16th century imperial architect, Mimar Sinan, suggests that the Ottomans also held similar ideas. "I saw the monuments, the great ancient remains. From every ruin I learned, from every building I absorbed something."[108] In this statement, Sinan is describing the act of reading the ancient past by physically visiting the sites of the ancient remains and learning from them. Therefore, just as Fontenelle relied on an ancient world for enlightenment, so too did Sinan, who was inspired by ideas from (his interpretation of) the Ottoman-Islamic version of "Truth and Beauty". Sinan's observations, in the above example and throughout his autobiographies, also resonate with those of the Renaissance humanists. For example, as in Alberti's treatise, where he argues that invention should not be *ex novo*—i.e., individuals "should strive to produce [their] own inventions, to rival, or, if possible to surpass the glory of theirs [i.e., past artists]"[109]—Sinan's *Treatise on Architecture* also references works (inventions) that are rich with architectural skill, perception, understanding and vision.[110] Sinan's treatise resonates with a humanist spirit, and participates in a parallel discourse with the Renaissance. It also connects his work with Islam, as can be seen in the following Qur'anic verse:

> 'And [have We not] built for you the seven firmaments', without architect or builder and without column or pier made apparent and manifest above the earth's pure face the green vault and spreading canopy of the heavens. And kneading water and clay, [He] created humankind, and by means of a cloak of excellence, rendered more distinguished and superior than [His] other creations.[111]

Sinan's references to God as the "Divine Architect" and as having created the world without any columns or other equipment, but fashioning Man and raising him above all other creations. By endowing him with special gifts and talents, Sinan alludes to the extraordinary skill and vision that architects, such as himself, needed to possess in order to create "artistic accomplishments."[112] Sinan's scribe, Sa'i, also implied that there was a parallel between the "Divine Architect" and Sinan, His "instrument", whose domed mosques represent the universe. The imagery in Sa'i's prose emphasises the quality of Sinan's mosques, that is, their status as 'Divine Creations' and symbols of God's wisdom. For example, Sa'i likens their columns and minarets to cypress trees, and the wavy patterns in their marble as ocean waves. He also describes their arches as reaching into the sky like rainbows; their domes as mountains that have been carved from the earth; their cupolas suspended like heavenly spheres, and their interior spaces and fountains as representations of the Gardens of Paradise.[113]

Sinan's autobiographies demonstrate a 16th century Ottoman Renaissance mindset of the humanist ethos, and are filled with reflections about fostering talented individuals in the service of the Sultan.[114]

They also demonstrate the Ottoman Islamic concept of the individual and his divine gifts, which should be used for the benefit of society. Sinan's humanist understanding of the divine gifts of individuals is deeply embedded in Islam. For example, Muslim philosophers who predated Sinan by several hundred years, such as Ibn Sina (d. 1037) and Ibn Rushd (1198) understood, as Pico (1463-1494) a Renaissance philosopher did, that "[t]here is nothing to be seen more wonderful than man."[115]

Renaissance material culture: hybrid connections

As a consequence of the trade and inter-cultural activities that were generated by Süleyman's conquests, Michael Rogers asserts that it "gave the arts in his reign a certain eclectic character which brings them close in spirit, though not always in effect, the arts at the Mannerist courts of Europe, Florence, Mantua, Fontainebleau and, slightly later, Prague."[116] Following these conquests craftsmen and artists like marble workers, carpenters, glaziers, masons and decorators from Cairo, Aleppo, Tabriz, Central Europe and the Balkans accompanied the Sultan back to Istanbul to transform the capital into a 'New Rome'.[117]

The conquests of Süleyman across Europe, Iran and the Eastern Mediterranean brought riches to his empire and his court. At the same time, however, these conquests stimulated diplomacy, trade and tributes, at levels that were unprecedented in Ottoman history. From the North, Poland and Muscovy, the Ottomans acquired luxurious goods like fur. From Venice, Genoa, Leghorn, Ancona and Ragusa came the finest wool, glass, and vast quantities of Venetian and Florentine velvets, brocades and other silk textiles. Silver poured in from South Germany, Transylvania, Ragusa and Venice[118]. In return for these goods, there was demand for Ottoman wares, such as Bursa silk, Ushak kilims, Iznik tiles and ceramics. Spices were also sent to Europe, and included diplomatic gifts for heads of state from the Venetian doges, as well as the tsars of Muscovy. Due to the impact and influence of these exchanges of material culture, flowing from East to West and West to East, impressions of Ottoman visual culture undoubtedly began to make its presence felt, and hybrid artworks that integrating Ottoman motifs became popular in the West.

In *Turkish Art*, Esin Atıl argues for the distinct and unique characteristics of Ottoman art in the Islamic world. She writes: "[t]he development of the art of the book, particularly of manuscript illustration traces the life-style of a society that evolved from a classical Islamic world into one that was uniquely Ottoman."[119] Atıl denies the assertions made about the patronage of Mehmed II of Italian artists; that the culture of Renaissance Italy was alien to the Ottomans, and as a consequence the Ottomans made no long-term contribution to European arts.[120] According to Atıl, "[...] the Ottoman impact on Renaissance Europe, is far more pronounced with an increased interest in Oriental motifs," from Anatolian kilims, velvets, silks, Iznik ware, gold and jewel-encrusted objects with intricate motifs and designs, came to play a significant role in Renaissance Italy, Northern and Eastern European artwork from the 15th to 17th centuries.[121] This is clearly evident in the objects housed in the museums of Europe, which imitate Ottoman motifs. For example, such cross-hybrid artworks include Hungarian embroidery of the early 17th century—its design reflects those of its Ottoman counterparts, and similar examples exist for Iznik ceramics and tiles, caftans and textile designs. Figure 3 depicts a large leaf-like motif that surrounds the middle decoration, and is topped with a carnation—its inspiration has Ottoman roots, i.e., the serrated *saz* leaf motif *(Figure 7)*. In another interesting embroidery—an altar cloth from the Abujvar Calvinist Church in Northern Hungary—also housed in the Hungarian National Museum in Budapest, one can see pseudo-Ottoman inscriptions, tulips, carnations, pomegranates, *saz* leaves with triple dots, and Chinese cloud motifs, which are all directly taken from Ottoman models *(Figure 8)*.

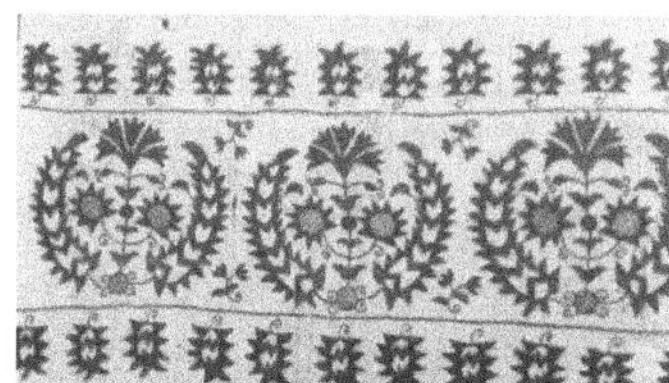

Figure 7. Hungarian embroidery after Ottoman designs with serrated saz leaves and carnations, early 17th century. Hungarian National Museum, Budapest. Photograph by Metin Mustafa, December, 2014.

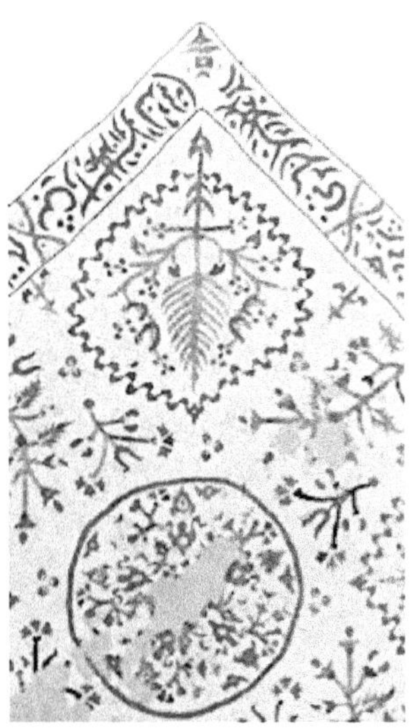

Figure 8. Embroidery, Hungarian, with Ottoman motifs and pseudo-Ottoman inscriptions along the border. Early 1600s, from the Abujvar Church. Hungarian National Museum, Budapest. Photograph by Metin Mustafa, December, 2014.

Poland also has its share of Ottoman-inspired artwork, due to its strengthening links with Hungary from 15th century onwards, which brought it closer to sharing a border with the Ottoman Empire. In fact, border sharing became one of the primary means by which Ottoman material culture entered and inspired local artisans of Europe. According to the Polish scholar, Dziewulski, during the reign of Bathory, Polish armour began to look more like Ottoman models. One of the reasons for this was to imitate the enemy's way of fighting and use of tactics. An example of such 'imitation' can be seen in a Polish hussar uniform housed at the Czartoryski Museum *(Figure 9)*. As Dziewulski, asserts the Polish regiments were modelled on the Ottoman *sipahi* (regular cavalry) and *deli* cavalry (frontier advance guard). As seen in Arifi's *Süleymanname* of 1558, the wings and wild-animal skins used in the uniforms of the Polish hussars were directly inspired by the feathers and skins used by the *deli* cavalrymen *(Figure 10)*.

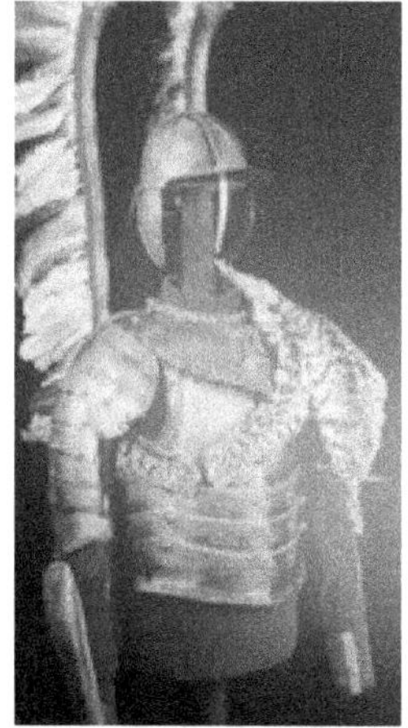

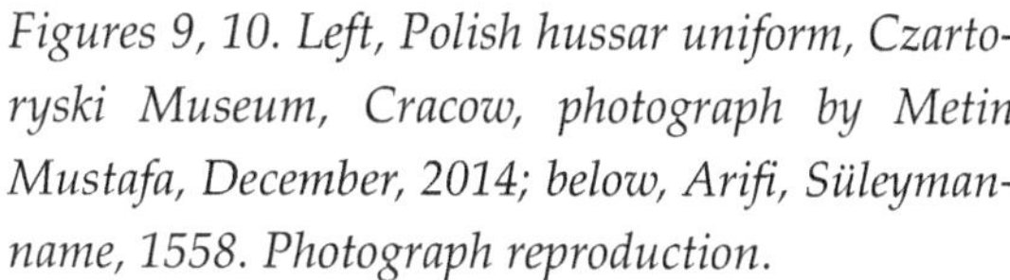

Figures 9, 10. Left, Polish hussar uniform, Czartoryski Museum, Cracow, photograph by Metin Mustafa, December, 2014; below, Arifi, Süleymanname, 1558. Photograph reproduction.

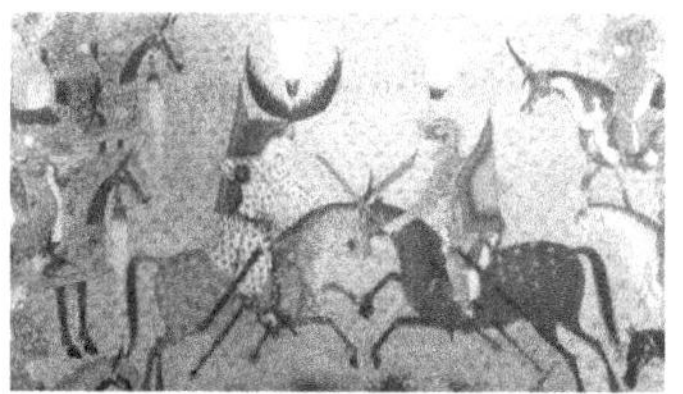

These blurred cross-representations of Ottoman imperial power, fashioned by the Eastern Europeans, is also evident in the richly embellished examples of Ottoman maces or *gürz,* such as winged maces (*şeşber*) *(Figures 11-13)*. These were used in Ottoman ceremonies and became popular among the European courts—not only as symbols of power but also for use in knightly tournaments. For example, figures dressed in Ottoman costumes, with arms and armour, depicted as part of the 1473 and 1669 Carnival of Rome, show Maria Marcini (the niece of Cardinal Mazarin) on the latter occasion, accompanied by 24 cavaliers dressed in Ottoman costumes and carrying Ottoman weapons.[122]

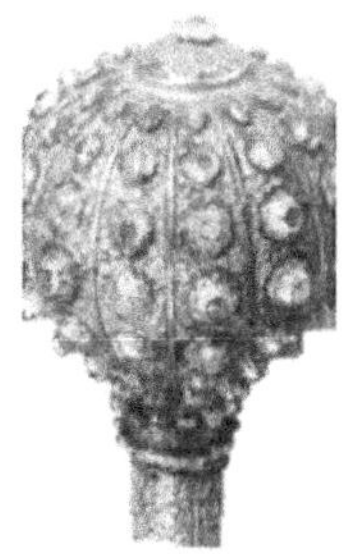

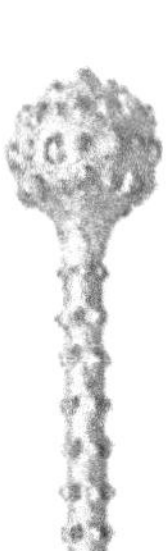

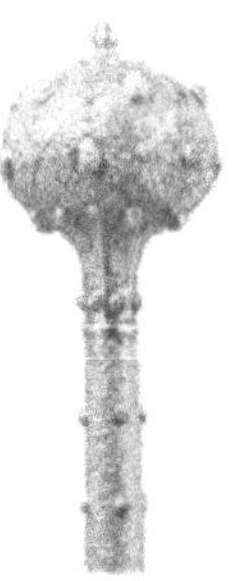

Figures 11, 12, 13. Left, Ottoman ceremonial mace, Topkapı Palace Museum; centre, ceremonial mace, Ottoman 17th century, Museum of Applied Arts, Budapest; right, ceremonial maces, European, 17th century, Kunsthistorisches Museum, Vienna. Photographs by Metin Mustafa, December 2014.

By imitating their Ottoman adversaries, European courts resembled that of the Sultan, who at the time, they still considered to be very intriguing and curious. Some examples of hybrid artwork were produced locally, and can be found in many museums around Europe —from Budapest to Moscow. However, these objects can also be found in formal portraits of central and eastern European nobility, where Ottoman-style spherical and winged maces were often used as symbols of power in Polish portraitures of nobility. *The Portrait of Janusz Radziwill* (Anonymous) is just one example, showing a Polish man in complete Ottoman-style outfit, including wearing a turban *(Figure 14).* There is no doubt that the image of the Turk played on the psyche of European artists. Ottoman visual culture was also emulated in the more northern parts of Europe. Pageantry and ceremonies were not exclusive to Renaissance Italy or Europe. Ottoman pomp and colourful costumes influenced the visual tastes of the courts of Europe, where the rulers came to emulate the sultans' courts. As Machiavelli advised those who would govern, "the great majority of mankind are satisfied with appearances, as though they were realities,

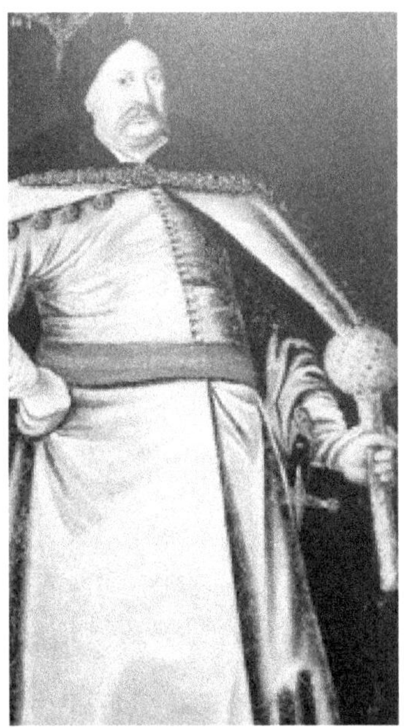

Figure 14. The Portrait of Janusz Radziwill, anonymous, c.1652. Royal Wavel Castle, Cracow. Eastern European nobility regularly carried both spherical and winged maces, which completed their Ottoman style outfits. Photograph by Metin Mustafa, December, 2014.

and are often even more influenced by things that seem than those that are."[123] It must be stated that from the onset of Ottoman military advances into the heart of Europe, from the late 14th century to the Second Siege of Vienna in 1683, their successive victories over Christendom contributed to mixed representations of the 'turbaned Turk' in Renaissance paintings. These representations, executed perhaps from defensive perspectives, nonetheless depict varied European readings of Ottoman invincibility. Often, representations of the 'turbaned Ottoman Turk' both fascinated and irritated a European audience, who saw the subjects as a "menace".[124]

Masked plays became popular in Renaissance Europe, during the 15th and 16th centuries when the threat of Turkish power was at its greatest. As a result of this, and perhaps as a coping mechanism of the elite, plays called *Mummereien* began depicting Turkish janissaries in masks and headdresses, which made them look like birds and other creatures —and were likely done to mock them. However, such scenes would later serve as part of an important prologue to the 'new Orientalism' that was a pan-European phenomenon of the 19th century (*Figures 15, 16*). As Ottoman power waned in the latter part of the 17th century, i.e., after 1683, Europe began to present a more respectful representation of Turks and regard almost every aspect of Ottoman material culture as worthy of adoption and emulation. Therefore, in addition to their desire for Ottoman goods, the European elite also took an interest in the ceremonial rituals and celebrations of the Ottoman Empire.

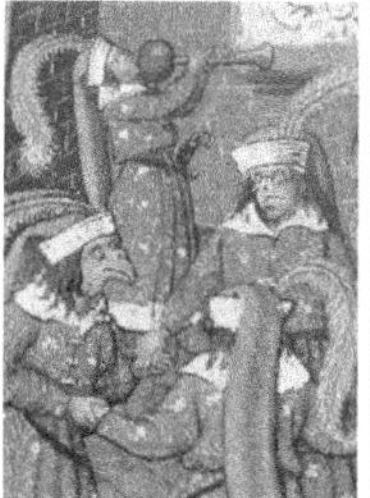

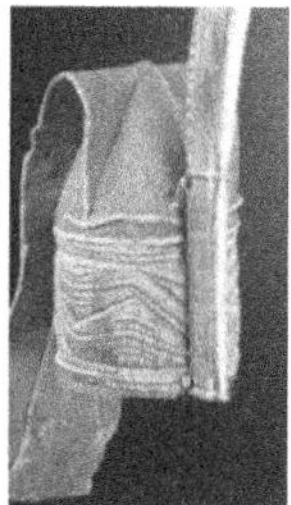

Figures 15, 16. Left, a masked play performance where actors are wearing bird masks with janissary headdresses. Engraving from the Turnierbuch Kaiser Maximilians I, 1515, Kunsthistorisches Museum, Vienna; right, Ottoman janissary headdress, 17th century, Kunsthistorisches Museum, Vienna. Photographs by Metin Mustafa, December 2014.

At other times it seemed better to emulate the Ottoman 'other' in ceremonial images, as seen in the 1607 *Book of Festivals* where Christian II (reign 1591-1611), Elector of Saxony. Christian II is shown dressed as an Ottoman sultan during the tournaments of 1607—an event at which people from various countries dressed in national costume. He was the first elector of Saxony to dress in sultan's attire and parade with his attendants in janissaries' costumes *(Figure 17).*

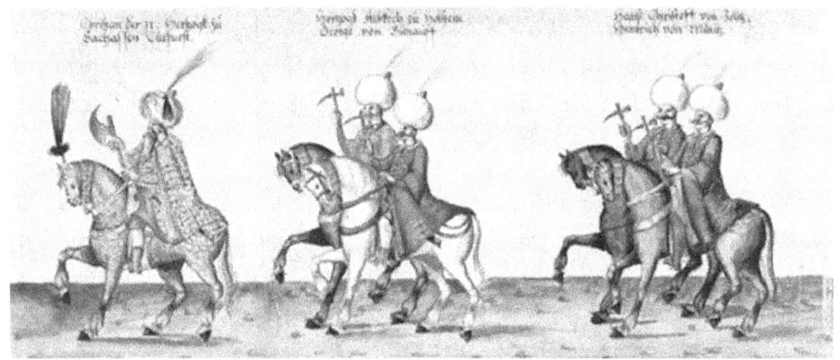

Figures 17. Christian II, Elector of Saxony as an Ottoman sultan with his attendants dressed in Ottoman costumes holding war hammers in their hands, anonymous, 1607, Fastnacht Manuscript (Book of Festivals). Photograph reproduction.

The representations of the image of the Turk throughout the period by painters in Italy and Northern Europe were painstakingly attempting to *include*—in a positive but cautious manner, rather than *exclude*—the Ottomans from the Renaissance visual narrative. In doing so, rather than obscuring our perceptions of the Renaissance, the blurred cultural boundaries make it clear that the Ottomans were an integral part of it.

Similarly, in Muscovy, Ottoman material culture made its presence felt through trade and diplomacy. This is apparent in many hybrid artworks, such as a Bible bound in Ottoman velvet with a typical, stylised, Ottoman carnation motif, and curtains that use nine lengths of Ottoman brocaded silk (*kemha*) with identical patterns of staggered rows of pomegranates, decorated with stylised tulips, carnations and hyacinths (but in atypical Ottoman colours so as to match the tastes of the tsarist court) *(Figure 18).*

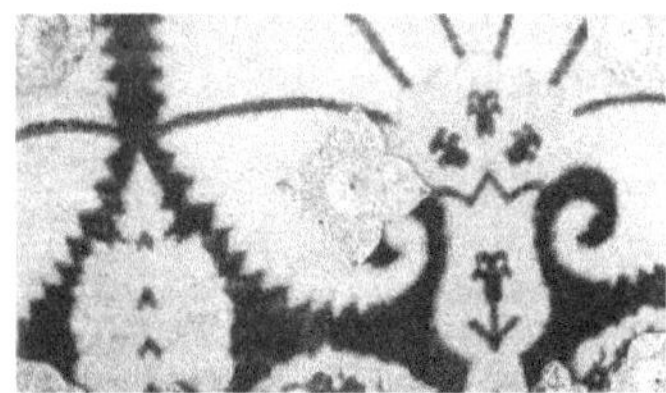

Figure 18. Bible bound in Ottoman velvet. 17th century, Kremlin Armoury Museum, Moscow. Photograph by Metin Mustafa, December, 2014.

Another Ottoman imitation can be seen in the 1551 prayer box of Ivan IV, in the Cathedral of the Dominion in the Kremlin, which is lined with Ottoman brocaded silk *(Figure 19).*

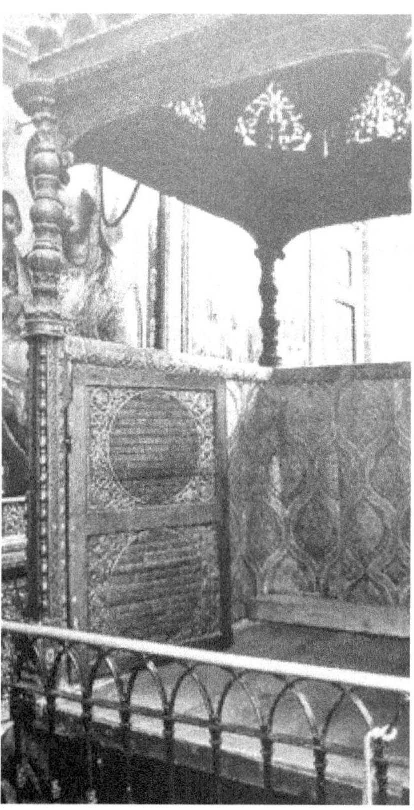

Figure 19. Prayer box of Ivan IV lined with Ottoman brocaded silk (kemha). The Cathedral of the Dominion, Kremlin, Moscow. Photograph by Metin Mustafa, December, 2014.

Likewise, an early 17th century Russian carriage consists of Ottoman brocaded velvet lining, which can be seen to cover the interior while the exterior decoration of the carriage consists of a star and rosette motif, and appears to have been based on Ottoman textile and Iznik designs *(Figures 20, 21).* The significance of these cultural exchanges demonstrates the veracity of the impact of Ottoman material culture in the courts, and local arts, of Eastern and Central Europe.

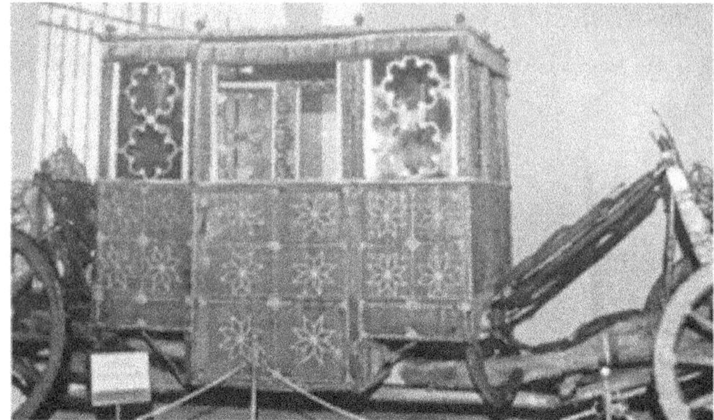
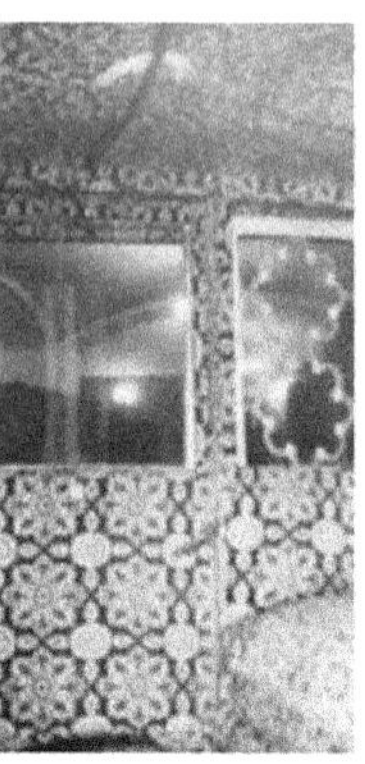

Figures 20, 21. Left, Russian carriage, 17th century. Kremlin Armoury Museum, Moscow, right, interior of the lining of the carriage depicting Ottoman brocaded velvet identical to many Ottoman textile designs. Photographs by Metin Mustafa, December, 2014.

When the notion of the renaissance is perceived from a revisionist perspective, and considers the numerous art objects found outside of Turkey—including silks, textiles, carpets, ceramics and jewelled pieces imitating Ottoman-Turkish motifs—and the museums in which they are housed, it remains somewhat of an enigma as to why Ottoman art continues to be neglected in the Western art theory of today. After all, hybrid artworks like those mentioned above, is readily found throughout Europe and also includes representations of Anatolian carpets in Venetian, English and Dutch paintings, and Iznik ceramics displayed in Venice, Naples and London museums—not to mention the various Ottoman-inspired exhibits in the Kremlin Armoury Chamber (Moscow), National Museum of Warsaw (Poland), Hungarian National Gallery, and the Museum of Applied Arts in Budapest, amongst other locations. Through this hybrid artwork and the accessibility of Ottoman material culture, which was made possible through commerce and diplomatic gift giving, eastern and western European artists and craftsmen were able to be inspired by one another. Additionally, the hybrid works of Russians, Poles, Hungarians, Italians, English and Dutch artisans, demonstrate the positive reception that Ottoman art was given by 16th century Europe. Therefore, the current research indicates that Ottoman material culture was very visible in Eastern Europe and the vassal states, and had a more lasting impact there than in Western Europe where Ottoman commodities were mostly in the form of display objects, such as Turkish *kilims* and Iznik ceramic wares. Similarly, Ottoman art provided sources of inspiration for surface decorations, but Ottoman customs and way of life were typically shared through the accounts of travellers. However, when the Ottomans granted trading rights to foreigners, they not only ensured the flow of goods in and out of the empire, but also allowed Ottoman objects of art to reach and influence the craftsmen of other lands.

Despite cross-cultural architectural and aesthetic parallels between Istanbul and Renaissance Italy, which can be seen in many monuments built in the 16th century, representing the 'Other' became a new genre in Renaissance art and, ironically, was largely influenced by the visual and material culture of the Ottomans. However, in spite of its positive Western reception in the 16th century, the importance of Ottoman visual culture is largely neglected today.

Representing the 'Other'

Due to its shared heritage with Western Europe, Ottoman cultural interactions and curiosity about the 'other' enabled both sides to observe and represent one another in art. Based on Paolo Giovio's prototype, Titian's portrait of the young Sultan Süleyman in 1539 depicts his intuitive, creative and "individualized face".[125] The portrait was made possible from coins, medals and verbal descriptions *(Figure 22).*[126] The Sultan also makes another appearance in Titian's *Ecce Homo* of 1543, where the features of Süleyman are used to represent a generic Ottoman figure, while in his *Pesaro Altarpiece* of 1519-26, Titian added a second turbaned bystander *(Figures 23, 23a, 24).*

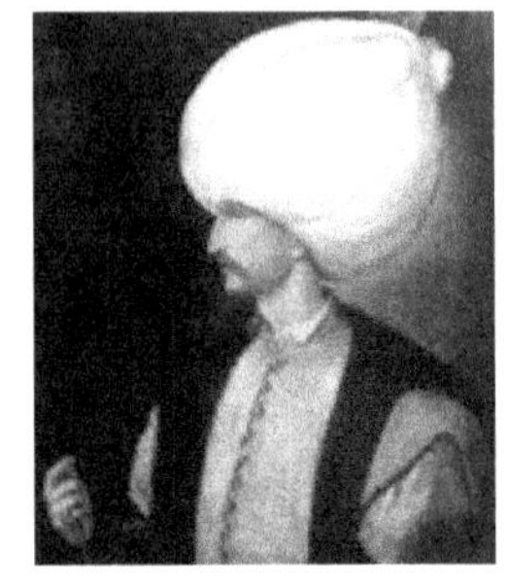

Figure 22. Portrait of Süleyman the Magnificent by Titian, c.1539. It is uncertain whether Titian painted the sultan with the four-tiered crown as it is not shown in the portrait. Photograph reproduction.

The same is also true in Brueghel's (1525-1569) *St John Preaching,* which shows the figure of an Ottoman standing among the crowd, and raises awareness of the increased diplomatic and commercial activities between the Ottomans and Italians in the 16th century. The inclusion of Ottoman figures in Italian Renaissance art signifies, not only a fascination with—and curiosity of—the 'other', but also demonstrates the interactions between the two cultures: diplomatically, economically, militarily and culturally.

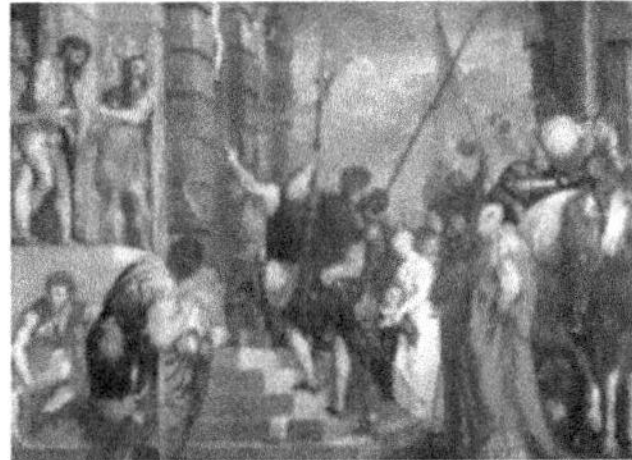

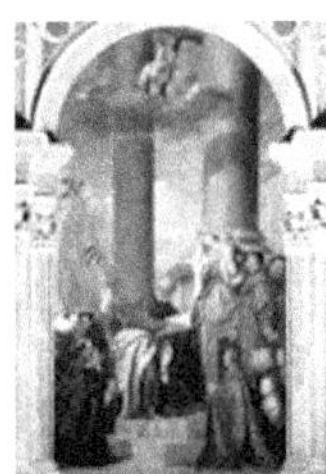

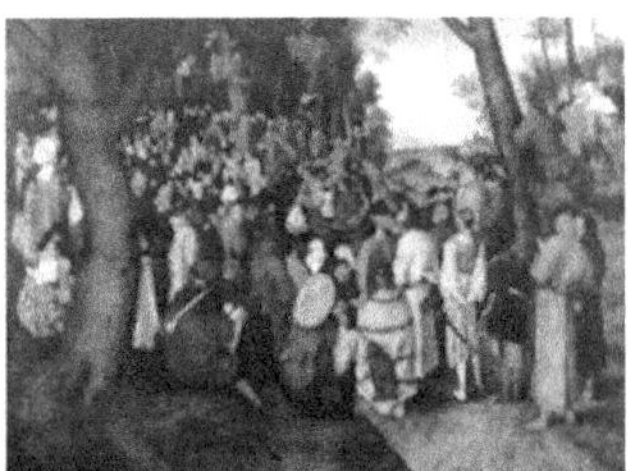

Figures 23, 23a, 24. Left, the sultan makes another appearance in Titian's Ecce Homo of 1543 where he uses the features of Süleyman simply to represent an Ottoman figure while in his Pesaro Altarpiece of 1519-26 (centre), he used a second turbaned bystander as seen on the left. Right, Brueghel's (1525-1569) St John Preaching the figure of an Ottoman standing among the crowd raises awareness of the increased diplomatic and commercial activities between the Ottomans and the Italians in the sixteenth century, Museum of Fine Arts, Budapest, Hungary. Photographs by Metin Mustafa, December, 2014.

In addition to creating a new painting genre in Renaissance Italy, i.e., one that depicted Ottoman figures and Anatolian carpets, the Ottoman art of Iznik ceramics also made a huge impact on Renaissance artisans. By the beginning in the 14th century, examples of Ottoman ceramics become abundant in Italy, and by the 17th and 18th centuries they are also seen in Holland in Delft production. Additionally, in France and England, Ottoman ceramics begin to appear in the 19th century, and by the early 20th century they can be found in Moscow.[127] According to Filiz Yenişehirlioğlu, in her article, "Ottoman Ceramics in European Contexts":

> In Italy, centers like Derruat, Farenza, Florence, Docia, and Naples either imitated or made exact copies of Ottoman plates; sixteenth-century Ottoman ceramic plates in Italian collections constituted the genuine exemplars from which reproduction could be made. The composition of flowers placed on both sides of a central leaf seems to have been a popular decorative scheme imitated on many majolica plates. Focusing on a specific type of floral decoration reminiscent of the *saz* style initiated by Nakkas Sahkulu, this composition seems to illustrate what was distinctively intended for the Italian market, since compositions with human animal figures, geometric patterns, or stylized palmette or half-palmette ornamentation were not reproduced. Such a specific choice was influential in European perception of the 'pure' Ottoman style as the floral style of the classical period.[128]

These motifs became the hallmark of Ottoman art and came to dominate the design patterns used on caftans, ceramics, tiles and silks

Just as 15th century European painters and artists, like Gentile Bellini and Costanzo de Ferrarro, at Mehmed II's court influenced contemporary Ottoman painters like Sinan Bey and Ahmed of Bursa in their representations of the sultan in Ottoman-Italian Renaissance mannerisms, so too, did the Ottoman artists in the *saz* style, initiated by Nakkaş Şahkulu, influence Italian ceramists to imitate the Ottoman style. The Italian ceramists on their majolica, as Yenişehirlioğlu has shown, "[...] not only reproduced exact copies of Ottoman plates but, following the tradition of Italian Renaissance painting, also included figural compositions as decorative theme in itself – mainly portraits of turbaned men or equestrian figures in Ottoman costume. These were popular subjects on *albarellos* produced in Sicily".[129] These cross-cultural exchanges of artistic influences are clear examples of the blurring of cultural boundaries—"[...] direct copies and imitations of original examples; sometimes the original features were reinterpreted and recreated in a different production technique; sometimes the circulation of both the original and their reproductions generated new and hybrid stylistic features among craftsmen of different cultural milieux."[130] At the same time, Italian merchants ordered textiles from Bursa while Italian glass was imported to Istanbul. As the Renaissance came to be defined more and more with luxurious and exotic goods that represented prestige and power of the princely courts, Ottoman silk and fine art of Iznik became integral commodities in the representation of Renaissance material culture.

Ottoman art was also influenced through Ottoman interactions with Venetian diplomats, and artists residing in Istanbul who collaborated with Ottoman artists. This was especially so through the diplomatic activities of Sokollu Mehmed Pasha and his Venetian counterpart in Istanbul, Marc'Antonio Barbaro—and his contact with the Florentine, Paolo Giovio (1483-1552). Giovio's illustrations of historical figures of the time, including 11 images of Ottoman sultans accompanied by complementary text, suggest a preoccupation with global interconnection. Giovio's text included carefully crafted textual treatments of the figures, and he subsequently composed brief eulogies to hang beneath each of the portraits, which suggests the precariousness of neutrality when dealing with the Ottoman 'other'. This genre had a great impact on Ottoman miniature paintings in the manuscripts of the latter part of the 16thcentury, such as *Semailname* (1579) and *Surname-i Hümayun* (1582), in which the *nakkashane* (imperial palace studio) artists of the palace integrated portraits of the sultans with accompanying descriptions.

CONCLUSION

The uniqueness of the 15th and 16th centuries and the Ottoman expansion into Europe demonstrated and increased contact between the East and West. Just as commercial goods travelled between the two regions, so too did cultural ideas and translations of power, pleasure, wealth, luxury, imitation, collecting and describing. All these factors held the potential for building the inter-cultural visual relationship between the two sides, and sum up the uniqueness of the parallel renaissances that occurred throughout the Mediterranean.

By considering what was occurring during the Renaissance in Italy and Europe at the time only serves to increase the importance of the Ottoman Empire's role in shaping certain fundamental aspects of this historical period in art. By negotiating the Renaissance, it is possible that two different cultural traditions—through commercial, diplomatic and military activities—produced parallel flowerings of artistic expressions; in some ways similar and in other ways unique to their own traditions. This convergence in the 16th century, especially between Istanbul, Venice, Poland, Muscovy and Hungary, became more evident during the economic, military and artistic zenith of the Ottoman Empire under Süleyman the Magnificent, his son Selim II and grandson Murad III. The term 'Renaissance' needs to remain a part of art history, in order to remind humanity that apart from its historical reality of the flowering of the arts in the 16th century Mediterranean, human creativity and beauty embraced cultural and religious diversity and produced something unique.

Bibliography

Abulafia, David. *The Great Sea: A Human History of the Mediterranean.* New York: Oxford University Press, 2011.

Adler, Friedrich. 'Die Moscheen zu Constantinopel: Eine architektonische baugeschictliche Studie,' (The Mosques of Constantinople: An Architectural Study), *Deutsche Bauzeitung* 8 (1874).

Alberti, Leon Batista. *On the Art of Building in Ten Books.* Edited by Joseph Rykwert, Neil Leach and Robert Tavenor. Cambridge MA and London: MIT Press, 1989.

Ali, Mustafa. *Epic Deeds of Artists.* Edited, translated and commented by Esra Akin-Kivanc. Leiden: Brill, 2011.

Atasoy, Nurhan. "Nakkaş Osman'ın Padişah Portreleri Albümü." *Türkiyemiz* 6 (1972): 2-12.

Atıl, E. "Art and Architecture." In *History of the Ottoman State, Society and Civilization,* II. Edited and preface by Ekmeleddin İhsanoğlu. Istan bul: IRCICA, 2002).

Atıl, Esin. 'The Image of Süleyman in Ottoman Art.' In *Süleyman the Second and His Time,* edited by Halil Inalcik and Cemal Kafadar, 333-341. Istanbul: The Isis Press, 2010.

Atıl, Esin. "Ottoman Miniature Painting under Sultan Mehmed II." *Ars Orientalis* Vol. 9 (1973): 103-120.

Atıl, Esin. *Süleymanname: The Illustrated History of Süleyman the Magnificent.* Washington: National Gallery of Art, 1986.

Atıl, Esin. *Turkish Art.* Washington and New York: Smithsonian Institution Press, 1980.

Avcıoğlu, N. "Istanbul: The Palimpsest City in Search of Its Architext." In *Anthropology and Aesthetics* 53-54 (Spring-Autumn, 2008): 190-210. Accessed March 25, 2015. http://www.jstor.org/stable/25608817194

Babinger, Franz. *Mehmed the Conqueror and His Time.* Translated by R. Manheim. Princeton: Princeton University Press, 1978.

Babinger, Franz. 'Die türkische Renaissance: Bemerkungen zum Schaffen des grossen türkischen Baumeisters Sinân.' *Beiträge zur Kenntnis des Orients* 9 (1914): 67–88.

Babinger, Franz. 'Ein osmanischer Michelangelo.' *Frankfurter Zeitung,* Sept. 7 (1915), no. 248.

Barkey, Karen. *Empire of Difference: The Ottomans in Comparative Perspective.* United Kingdom: Cambridge University Press, 2008.

Besnier-Kılıçoğlu, Selda. "Sinan and Palladio: The Parallel development of two master-builders." Accessed June 14, 2015. http://unesdoc.unesco.org/images/0007/000781/078126eo.pdf#77905, 34.

Bhabha, Homi. *The Location of Cultures.* London & New York: Routledge, 1994. Kindle edition.

Bisaha, Nancy. *Creating East West: Renaissance Humanists and the Ottoman Turks.* Philadelphia: University of Pennsylvania Press, 2006.

Borghesi, F., M. Papio and M. Riva, eds. *Pico Della Mirandola: Oration on the Dignity of Man, A New Translation and Commentary.* New York: Cambridge University Press, 2012.

Boyar, Ebru and Kate Fleet. *A Social History of Ottoman Istanbul.* United Kingdom: Cambridge University Press, 2010.

Braudel, Fernand. *The Mediterranean and the Mediterranean World in the Age of Philip II,* Vol. VI. London: Fontana Press, 1987.

Brotton, J. *The Renaissance: A Very Short Introduction.* New York: Oxford University Press, 2006.

Casale, Giancarlo. *The Ottoman Age of Exploration.* Oxford, New York: Oxford University Press, 2010.

Coles, Paul. *The Ottoman Impact on Europe.* London: Thames and Hudson, 1968.

Clot, Andre. *Suleiman the Magnificent.* London: Saqi, 2005.

Çötellioğlu, Ayşe. *Topkapı Palace Museum collection of paintings and Portraits of the Sultans.* Istanbul: Bilkent Kültür Girişimi Publications, 2012.

Dalrymple, William. "Foreword: The Process of Frontiers of Islam and Christendom: A Clash or Fusion of Civilisations?" In *Re-Orienting the Renaissance: Cultural Exchanges with the East,* edited by G. MacLean, ix-xxiii. New York: Palgrave, 2005.

Diez, Ernst. *Türk Sanatı: Başlangıcından Günümüze Kadar.* Translated by Oktay Aslanapa. Istanbul: Üniversite Matbaası, 1946.

Eilouti, Buthayna. "Sinan and Palladio: Two Cultures and Nine Squares." *International Journal of Architectural Heritage: Conservation, Analysis, and Restoration* 6, 1 (2011): 1-18. Accessed June 29, 2015. DOI: 10.1080/15583058.2010.495821.

Goody, J. *Renaissances: The One or the Many?* New York: Cambridge University Press, 2010.

Gurlitt, Cornelius. *Istanbul'un Mimari Sanatı, Architecture of Constantinople, Die Baukunst Konstantinopels*. Translated by Rezan Kızıltan, Ankara. Enformasyon ve Dokumantasyon Hizmetleri Vakfı, 1999.

Hale, Sheila. *Titian: His Life.* UK: Harper Collins, 2012. Accessed August 11, 2015. http://books.google.com.au/books?

Halman, Talat S. *Rapture and Revolution: Essays on Turkish Literature.* New York: Syracuse University Press, New York, 2007.

Howard, Deborah. *Venice and the East, The Impact of the Islamic World in Venetian Architecture 1100-1500.* New Haven and London: Yale University Press, 2000.

Inalcık, Halil. *The Ottoman Empire: The Classical Age 1300-1600.* London: Phoenix, 1994.

Itzkowitz, Norman. *Ottoman Empire and Islamic Tradition.* Chicago: University of Chicago Press, 1980.

Jardine, Lisa and Jerry Brotton. *Global Interest: Renaissance Art Between East and West.* London: Reaktion Books, 2000.

Jardine, Lisa. *Worldly Goods: A New History of the Renaissance.*London: W. W. Norton & Company, 1996.

Kafadar, C. *Between Two Worlds: The Construction of the Ottoman State.* Berkeley: University of California Press, 1995.

Karpat, Kemal & Yetkin Yıldırım. *The Ottoman Mosaic: Preservation of minority groups, Religious tolerance, Governance of Ethnically diverse societies.* Seattle: Cune Press, 2010.

Kinross, Lord. *The Ottoman Centuries - The Rise and Fall of the Turkish Empire.* U.S: Quill, 1990.

Kostof, Spiro. *A History of Architecture: Settings and Rituals.* New York: Oxford University Press, 1985.

Lewis, Bernard. *Cultures In Conflict: Christian, Muslim, and Jews in the Age of Discovery.* New York: Oxford University Press, 1995.

Lewis, Raphaela. *Everyday Life on Ottoman Turkey.* UK: Dorset, 1988.

MacClean, Gerald. "Introduction: Re-Orienting the Renaissance." In *Re-Orienting the Renaissance,* edited by Gerald MacClean, 1-28. New York: Palgrave Macmillan, 2005.

Machiavelli, Niccolo. *The Prince and the Discourses.* Translated by Luigi Ricci. New York: Modern Library College, 1950.

Mack, Rosamond E. *Bazaar to Piazza: Islamic Trade and Italian Art, 1300-1600.* California: University of California, 2002.

Mansel, P. *Constantinople: City of the World's Desire, 1453-1924.* London: John Murray, 1996.

Matthews, Henry. "Rethinking Ottoman Architecture." Paper presented at the ACSA International Conference, 2001.

Muir, E. "Images of Power: Art and Pageantry in Renaissance Venice." *American Historical Review* 84 (1979): 16-52.

Muir, E. "Representations of Power." In *Italy in the Age of Renaissance.* Edited by

John M. Najemy, 226-245. New York: Oxford University Press, 2009.

Mustafa, Metin. "Iconography of Renaissance ceremonials in the Early Modern World." *Australian Journal of Islamic Studies* 3, 1 (2018): 1-23.

Mustafa, Metin. *The Ottoman Renaissance: A Reconsideration of Early Modern Ottoman Art 1413-1575.* New Jersey: Blue Dome Press, 2018.

Najemy, John M. *Italy in the Age of the Renaissance 1300-1550.* New York: Oxford University Press, 2004.

Necipoğlu, Gulru. *The Age of Sinan: Architectural Culture in the Ottoman Empire.* London: Reaktion Books, 2005.

Necipoğlu, Gülru. "From Byzantine Constantinople to Ottoman Konstantiniyye: Creation of a Cosmopolitan Capital and Visual Culture Under Sultan Mehmed II." In *From Byzantium to Istanbul: 8000 Years of Capital,* edited by Nazan Ölçer, 265-276. Istanbul: Sabancı University, Sakip Sabancı Museum, 2010.

Necipoğlu, Gülru and Alina Payne, eds. *Histories of Ornament: From Global to Local.* Princeton: Princeton University Press, 2016.

Norton, Claire. "Blurring the Boundaries: Intellectual and Cultural Interaction between Eastern and Western: Christian and Muslim Worlds." In *The Renaissance and the Ottoman World,* edited by Anna Contadini and Claire Norton, 3-22. England: Ashgate Publishing Limited, 2013.

Ousterhout, Robert. "The East, the West, and the Appropriation of the Past in Early Ottoman Architecture," Vol, 43, no. 2 (2004): 165-176. *International Center of Medieval Art.* Accessed March 24, 2015. http://www.jstor.org/stable/25067103.

Qur'an

Raby, John. "A Sultan of Paradox: Mehmed the Conqueror as a patron of the art." *Oxford Art Journal,* Vol. 5, No. 1, Patronage (1982): 3-8. Accessed May 15, 2015. http://www.jstor.org/stable/1360098.

Rogers, M. "The Arts Under Süleyman the Magnificent." In *Süleyman the Second and His Time,* edited by H. Inalcık and C. Kafadar. Istanbul: The Isis Press, 2010.

Ross, James Bruce and Mary M. McLaughlin, eds. *The Portable Renaissance Reader.* New York: Penguin Books, 1977.

Sa'i, Mustafa. *Sinan's Autobiographies: Five Sixteenth Century Texts.* Introductory Notes, Critical Editions, and Translations by Howard Crane and Esra Akin, edited by Gülru Necipoğlu. Leiden: Brill, 2006.

Said, Edward. *Orientalism.* London: Penguin Books, 1995.

Sardar, Z. *Orientalism.* Buckingham: Open University Press, 1999.

Sewell, Brian. "Sinan: The Architect of a Forgotten Renaissance." *Cornucopia*, 1992/93.

St. Clair, Alexandrine N. "Turkengefahr." In *Islamic Art in the Metropolitan Museum*. Edited by Richard Ettinghausen, 315-34. New York: Metropolitan Museum of Art, 1972.

Stamoulos, E. *Mehmed II's Portraits: Patronage, Historiography and the Early Modern Context*. Montreal: McGill University, 2005.

The Age of Süleyman the Magnificent. New South Wales, Australia: Art Exhibitions Australia / Beagle Press, 1990, Exhibition Publication.

Wittkower, R. *Architectural Principles in the Age of Humanism*. New York: W. W. Norton & Company Inc., 1972.

Yenişehirlioğlu, Filiz. "Ottoman Ceramics in European Contexts." *Muqarnas*, Vol. 21 (2004): 373-382. Accessed August 29, 2015. http://www.jstor.org/discover/10.2307/1523369?

Yerasimos, S. *Constantinople: Istanbul's Historical Heritage*. Paris: H. F. Ullmann Publishing, 2012.

Yurdaydın, H. G. *Matrakçi Nasuh*. Ankara: Türk Tarih Kurumu, 1963.

The Iconography of Renaissance Ceremonials in the Early Modern World

ESSAY III

INTRODUCTION

The iconography of Renaissance festivals and ceremonies came to reflect early modern political, social and cultural representations of dynastic identity and power in Europe and the Ottoman Empire. *Imitazione* (imitation) and *adeguazione* (adaptation) of the past into contemporary contexts underpin the 16th century Vasarian understanding of *rinascita* (rebirth).[1] This Renaissance paradigm of cultural awakening exemplifies the iconography of Ottoman and Italian ceremonies and characterises the complex and culturally inclusive nature of the early modern period. As Mulryne, Aliverti and Testaverde state:

> Festivals were interdisciplinary and, on occasion, international in scope. They drew on a rich classical heritage and developed a shared pan-European iconography as well as exploiting regional and site-specific features. They played an important part in local politics and the local economy, as well as international negotiations and the conscious presentation of power, sophistication and national identity.[2]

Whether set against the background of St. Mark's Square in Venice and the Byzantine-inspired St. Mark's cathedral with the bronze horses taken from Constantinople during the Fourth Crusade (1202-1204), or the At Meydanı (old Roman Hippodrome) in Ottoman Istanbul, these pageants and ceremonies demonstrated power, identity and courtly magnificence of respective rulers. As Matteo Burioni questions: "Is there just one concept of rebirth, or should we account for a wider variety of instances of rebirth"[3] Similarly, Jerry Brotton's assertion of a "... more global perspective on the nature of the Renaissance" is needed where a series of "Renaissances throughout the regions, each with their own highly specific and separate characteristics ... overlapped and exchanged influences with the more classical and traditionally understood Renaissance centred on Italy."[4]

This international scope allows a more culturally inclusive Renaissance narrative of the rebirth of cultural magnificence and reawakening by engaging with the classical past, and one that includes the Ottoman Empire. The influence of early modern Ottoman visual expressions on the courts of Renaissance Italy realigns and re-orients the language of the iconography of pageants and ceremonies. Through their aural, visual, literary and theatrical features, including costuming and setting aesthetics like carpets, the pageants and ceremonies underscore the *Ottomanising* influence found within the pluralistic Renaissance context of the Mediterranean basin in the 16th century.[5]

This paper investigates the 1582 Ottoman celebration of Murad III's son's circumcision depicted in the illuminated manuscript, *Surname-i Hümayun*. By comparing this event to Renaissance ceremonies, one sees very little separating the ceremonies of East and West in purpose or aesthetics. In fact, in some European ceremonies and pageants, a hybrid art form emerged, where imitations of Ottoman art objects – influenced by diplomatic relations and trade – blurred the cultural boundaries of Ottoman and European Renaissances. Typically set before an audience of foreign guests, such spectacles were major contributors to the composition and circulation of Ottoman costume books, which depicted 16th century daily life in the Sultan's capital and increased the dissemination of Ottoman visual culture throughout Renaissance Italy, Saxony and Poland.[6]

Visual impressions of lavish ceremonies in Renaissance Italy were captured through their own courtly observations, including processions in Florence and processions through St. Mark's Square in Venice. Similarly, the Ottoman court used manuscripts to depict, and preserve, the histories of events such as post-battle marches of triumphant Sultans returning to Istanbul, weekly Friday prayer processions and the circumcision ceremonies of royal princes.

Methodology

This article examines the cultural mimicry that existed between the two early modern societies and how it defined the complex and multinational Renaissance identity. If the Ottoman court and its European counterparts shared similarities in visual taste and ceremony, can the pageants during the reign of Sultan Süleyman the Magnificent be considered part of the Renaissance experience of cultural awakening and magnificence? And, according to Orientalism discourse, why was there a desire in Europe to imitate the Ottoman 'Other'?[7]

Renaissance dukes and princes, using visual representations of themselves as well as emulating their adversaries, resorted to mimicry. Their act of constructing reality was influenced by "things that seem [rather] than those that are."[8] Cultural theorist Homi Bhabha argues mimicry is a desire to recognise the 'Other' as a "subject of a difference that is almost the same, but not quite."[9] For Bhabha, it represents,

---

> [...] a difference that is itself a process of disavowal. Mimicry is, thus the sign of a double articulation; a complex strategy of reform, regulation and discipline, which 'appropriates' the Other as it visualises power.[10]

The desire to assert their (i.e., Florence and Venice) power and identity by imitating the Ottoman 'Other' may have been a symbolic way of accepting their nemesis into the Renaissance discourse. However, the problematic nature of their imitation through the "sign of a double articulation" had more to do with marginalising the power of the Ottoman Empire while asserting its own supremacy. Through the desire to emerge from these representations of Ottoman ceremonies through mimicry, one is faced with the irony of "partial presence"—an "incomplete" identity—as a result of cultural deficiency.[11] According to Bhabha, their presence and representations of reality are twofold: "while one considers reality as it is [i.e. to be like the Ottomans] the other [i.e. to remain European] disavows it and replaces it by appropriating its desire that repeats and rearticulates 'reality' as mimicry."[12]

The desire of the courts of Renaissance Italy to imitate Ottoman ceremonies is related to "metonym of presence"; that is, where the identity of Renaissance courts through repetition also become 'different' like the Ottomans.[13] By crossing cultural boundaries and "enunciate[ing] through a strategic confusion of ... metaphoric and metonymic axes" the ceremonies represented "cultural production[s] of meaning."[14] In other words, Renaissance pageants and their mimicry of Ottoman culture was not due to mockery, but a desire to incorporate it as an active player and *metonymically* accept its 'Otherness' through a visual manifestation. The influence of the Ottomans' visual aesthetics on Renaissance ceremonial aesthetics of Italy definitely enriched and integrated the splendour and magnificence of these spectacles with an Eastern flavour.

THE CONTEXT OF OTTOMAN RENAISSANCE CEREMONIALS

The pageants of Süleyman the Magnificent (1520-1566), and those of Murad III (1574-1595), were held before international audiences, where stories about them spread across Europe. Pomp and ceremony were integral elements of Ottoman court culture, and the splendour of the Sultan and his household were used to impress the citizens of Istanbul. During a triumphant entry into the city by a victorious sultan, like Süleyman the Magnificent – as depicted in many of Peter Coeck's engravings – to the birth of a royal son, accession to the throne, imperial wedding of a sultan, pasha or princess, and the circumcision of a prince, the city became like the "centre of the universe."[15] As 17th century court poet Nedim wrote:

> O city of Istanbul, priceless and peerless! I would sacrifice all Persia for one of your stones![16]

The inhabitants of Istanbul connected with their city through the iconography of Renaissance ceremonies and pageants, regardless of whether they were secular or religious.

Ottoman ceremonies often used the old Roman Hippodrome (*At Meydanı* in Turkish) and the waters of the Bosphorus as their backdrop, which also included the Sultan's elegant narrow *kayıks* with their long-pointed prows, which were as iconic of Istanbul as gondolas were of Venice. Merging the classical past with a contemporary setting allowed the Ottomans to engage in the Renaissance discourse. The festivities were embellished with entertainment provided by chariot races, jugglers, simulated combat between janissaries, knights in armour and competitions in which Qur'anic verses were recited – all of which connected the city and dynasty to their classical roots. Lavish presents of crystal, Chinese porcelain, Syrian damask, muslin from India and slaves from Africa were presented to the Sultan by his pashas and viziers, and displayed to the public while poets recited works that had been composed in honour of the occasion. In return, the Sultan would present *hil'ats* (i.e. Ottoman kaftans) to his foreign guests and it was visual displays such as these that left European visitors with a cultural impression of Istanbul, which they then took back to Europe. In 1671, after observing one of the Sultan's processions when he left the palace to go hunting in Edirne, the French ambassador, Marquis de Nointel, wrote:

> If this ceremony has some splendour, one must take guard not to be overwhelmed by it ... The true remedy to avoid being prejudiced is to think of the grandeur of the King's [Louis IV] Household ... His Majesty wanting to make an entry, can efface without difficulty the finest spectacles in these regions and in the rest of the Levant.[17]

No other capital city in Europe produced such grand spectacles more often than Istanbul.[18] The combination of the visible beauty of the city, with its gleaming domed mosques and palaces—during the day—and its silhouetted minarets—at night—as well as the majesty of Topkapı Palace, ensured imperial processions and their splendour became an integral part of the Süleymanic Age and left lasting impressions on the visual culture of the early modern world.

Ottoman Pageants: Classical Past meets Ottoman Present

During the Sultanate of Süleyman and his successors (Selim II and Murad III), one of the implicit ways they demonstrated imperial authority was through iconic image ceremonies, which were spatially supported and elaborated by the architecture of the palace grounds. Selecting the location for a royal ceremony was a crucial part of preparing for it, and often involved appropriating settings that featured in classical antiquity. For example, the Roman Hippodrome in Istanbul played an integral role in Ottoman and Orientalised European ceremonies. In 1582, the *millet* (i.e. ethnic) groups of the Ottoman Empire, as depicted in *Surname-i Hümayun*—and included former slaves who had become pages, as well as eunuchs, pashas and viziers of the sultan's household—attended a 52-day (and night) festival at the Hippodrome. While this setting was not new to Ottoman ceremonies—as witnessed half a century earlier by the weddings of Sultan Süleyman to his wife Hürrem Sultan, and his Grand Vizier Ibrahim Pasha to the Sultan's sister Hatice Sultan—no illustrated manuscripts exist in relation to its earlier Ottoman history. However, according to contemporary historian Selaniki (d. 1600), as part of the preparations for the ceremony, the palace of Ibrahim Pasha was renovated with an additional high balcony and a new entrance in one corner.[19] Additionally, none of the statues that had been added by Ibrahim Pasha—from his campaign in Hungary earlier in the century—adorned the Hippodrome in front of the palace.

In 1582, Murad III commissioned the *Surname-i Hümayun* for his son's (Prince Mehmed) circumcision festival. This festival lasted for 52 days and was probably one of the grandest and most elaborate festivals the Ottomans ever held. Such events took months of preparation and included: the design and construction of pavilions, which required numerous trades and industries; organising large groups of people from all classes for public ceremonies to foreign dignitaries; arranging accommodation for such guests; and feeding several thousands of guests that would attend each day. Preparations began a year in advance and included everything from sending invitations to preparing the daily menus, which were organised by Kara Halil Bey (the superintendent of the imperial kitchens). Murad III made sure it was well-documented by the author Intizami, who worked chronologically to capture the details of events as they occurred, while court artists followed his written word to create accompanying miniatures.[20] As the guilds' floats passed by, and paraded their arts and crafts—watched by the Sultan from the palace of Ibrahim Pasha—Intizami appears to have captured every detail so viewers of the manuscript feel just as welcome at the event as the foreign guests who watched from the galleries. This visual expression reinforces Ottoman cultural self-awareness and interest. The documentary-style genre and recognition of history exemplify the Ottoman Renaissance mindset and one that equally engages in the Vasarian paradigm of *rinascita,* as noted above.

This manuscript, however, is more than a parade of the guilds of the empire. It challenges one of the main misconceptions about the non-celebratory status of Ottoman artists, which have contributed to the lack of receptivity of Ottoman art in the West. What it clearly demonstrates is the celebration of collective genius rather than that of individual genius, which clearly sets Ottoman artists apart from their

Florentine counterparts expressed by Giorgio Vasari in his work *The Lives of the Artists* (1550).

Throughout all of the manuscript's folios, the At Meydanı (old Hippodrome) features as part of the backdrop and in front of the Ibrahim Pasha Palace. Here, the Sultan, the Prince, members of the *harem* and other important guests are positioned. The At Meydanı features a Serpent Column that depicts three serpents, which originally stood in the Temple of Apollo at Delphi—symbolising the defeat of the Persians in the Battle of Plataea (479 BCE). It also houses an Egyptian Obelisk that had been built for Pharaoh Thutmose III (ca. 1500 BCE) as a means of recording his Syrian campaigns and crossing of the Euphrates; however, it was eventually brought to Constantinople in the fourth century because an emperor, perhaps Constantine, thought it could be a symbol of imperial power for the Hippodrome.

These classical allusions did not escape the literary elite of the Ottoman court. In fact, using the old Hippodrome as a theatrical setting for the circumcision festival—with the building's classical monuments from Ancient Greece and Egypt, and the fact its presence in Istanbul was due to an Eastern Roman emperor—produced a uniquely Ottoman Renaissance experience. Such visual expressions, linking the classical past within the Ottoman cultural and historical contexts, interweaved Ottoman celebrations into the 16th century Renaissance narrative that was taking place at the time. In particular, Prince Mehmed's (Süleyman's son) circumcision ceremony in 1530 was not only the first time a spectacle of its magnitude had been seen, it was also a very clever way in which the Ottomans appropriated and connected with the classical past. It asserted the self-fashioning and power of the imperial identity through engaging with their inherited heritage of the East and classical West. According to Necipoğlu, "[D]isplayed as parade accessories and stage props in ostentatious ceremonies, these ... royal status symbols were primarily aimed at communicating Ottoman imperial claims to a Europeans audience through a Western discourse of power."[21] Such grandiose ceremonies as visual expressions of power and courtly splendour represented dynastic self-fashioning during the Renaissance and reinforced the Ottomans' integral part in the discourse.

Influence of Ottoman visual culture on Renaissance Italy

Ottoman ceremonies and pageants became so popular that the courts of European dukes and princes began to emulate them. During the 16th and 17th centuries, Ottoman visual material culture became an integral part of European court ceremonies, in which Ottoman costumes and objects—that had been looted during the Battle of Lepanto—began to appear in pageants and as diplomatic gifts between European monarchs symbolising power, authority and even colonial possibility. For example, in 1587, Italian dukes sent a delegation, bearing gifts, to Saxony. The gifts came from the war booty of Lepanto and included an Ottoman helmet, and Italian imitations of Ottoman objects, such as a leather bow and quiver set featuring a coat of arms *(Figures 1 and 2).*

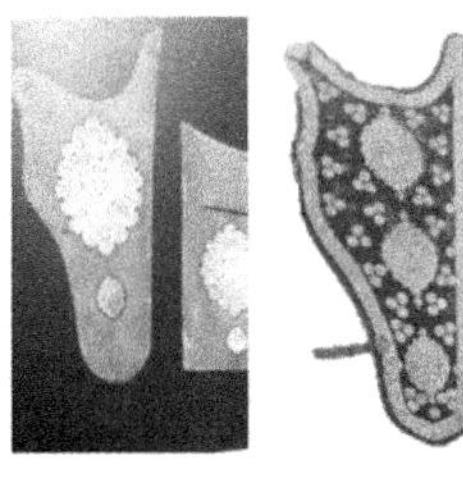

Figures 1 and 2. Left, a set of tirkeş or quiver and bow case or sadak, Italian, leather, mid-sixteenth century. Gifts made by the Italian delegation to the Elector in 1587 emulating Ottoman models as seen on the right; Left, Staatliche Kunstsammlungen, Rüstkammer, Dresden. Right, Topkapı Palace Museum, Istanbul. Photograph reproductions.

The use of Ottoman or Ottoman-inspired objects as gifts and in pageants was likely due to their connection with the exotic Eastern 'Other', which Saslow has expressed as:

> The iconography of the events – characters and their actions, whether embodied by artistic images, by public figures, on the urban stage, or by actors in frank impersonation – constitutes a revealing summation of the taste, imagery, and political symbolism of an influential late mannerist court.[22]

The thirst for Ottoman objects and visual aesthetics reinforces Bhaba's assertions above. Such practices contribute to a more culturally inclusive approach to the Renaissance discourse than previously thought.

Renaissance Wedding Ceremonies: The Medicis meet Süleyman the Magnificent

The depiction of a royal wedding shows it was also an occasion that attracted visual splendour in the streets of Istanbul, so the presence of imperial women could not be ignored. Süleyman's favourite concubine, Roxelana, as she was known to the Europeans, but named Hürrem by Süleyman because of her laughter, became the Ottoman 'queen' upon their marriage. A marriage like theirs was the first of its kind and Süleyman's unprecedented act constituted a break from the earlier traditions of the dynasty, which meant the dynastic family now focussed more on Istanbul than on the provinces of the Empire. Additionally, the importance of the *haseki* meant the husbands of these Ottoman princesses generated much prestige for the royal family, as evidenced by Princess Mihrimah's (daughter of Süleyman) marriage to Grand Vizier Rustem Pasha, and Süleyman's sister, Hatice Sultan, marrying Ibrahim Pasha (who was Rustem Pasha's predecessor). However, it appears no concubine received as much attention as Hürrem. Her title as *haseki* of Süleyman added to her status, but her marriage to Süleyman further promoted her ascendancy among the ruling elite.

The visual display of pomp and ceremony of the wedding would have very obviously marked Hürrem's elevation to 'Sultan' status. The marriage of Süleyman and Hürrem is clearly described by a representative of the Genoese Bank of St. George, in a letter in which he establishes the importance that such visual spectacles held for Ottoman audiences.[23] Through the medium of the marriage ceremony, Süleyman not only created a visual expression of his love for Hürrem, but also made a statement about his queen—his equal—and her identity as a woman of the ruling elite. According to the English ambassador to Constantinople, George Young witnessing the ceremony:

> This week there has occurred in this city a most extraordinary event, one absolutely unprecedented in the history of the Sultans. The Grand Signior Suleiman has taken to himself as his Empress a

> slave-woman from Russia, called Roxalana, and there has been great feasting. The ceremony took place in the Seraglio, and the festivities have been splendid beyond all record. There was a public procession of the presents. At night the principal streets are gaily illuminated, and there is much music and feasting. The houses are festooned with garlands and there are everywhere swings in which people swing by the hour with great enjoyment. In the old Hippodrome a great tribune is set up, the place reserved for the Empress and her ladies screened with a gilt lattice. Here Roxalana and the Court attended a great tournament in which both Christian and Moslem Knights were engaged, and tumblers and jugglers and a procession of wild beasts, and giraffes with necks so long they as it were touched the sky ... There is great talk about the marriage and none can say what it means.[24]

For the Venetian ambassador, Daniello De'Ludovici, the wedding occurred around June 1534.[25] While there are no miniatures that depict the actual event, there are a number of miniatures from during and after Süleyman's rule that can be pieced together to illustrate the visual spectacle that would have been displayed for his subjects. The appropriation of the Roman Hippodrome as a wedding backdrop set the stage for the merging of classical aesthetics with Ottoman visual tastes, which was interspersed with Muslim and Christian entertainment, and further signified the interconnectedness of the two Renaissance civilisations.

The pomp of such ceremonies was, of course, not exclusive to the Ottoman court. Similar marriage festivities were also seen in 16th century Venice, for in Renaissance Italy, just as in the Ottoman Empire, the "theme[s] of marriage, and of love and virtue within marriage"[26] were deemed worthy of pageantry. In Renaissance Italy, the marriage of the elite used decorative and entertaining effects: "jousts and historical or recounted battles were good subjects for a display of the chivalric paraphernalia which became increasingly fashionable during the century."[27] In 1539, at around the same time as Süleyman and

Hürrem's marriage, stories of the magnificent scenery and floats used at the wedding of the great Cosimo I de' Medici (1519-1574) and Eleonora di Toledo are well known through Giorgio Vasari's *Lives* (1550), as well as through other sources. In Vasari's account of the life of the resourceful designer Il Tribolo, Vasari describes the wedding that took place in Florence:

> Tribolo was given the charge of constructing a triumphal arch at the Porta al Prato, through which the bride, coming from Poggio, was to enter; which arch he made a thing of beauty, very ornate with columns, pilasters, architraves, great cornices, and pediments. The arch was to be all covered with figures and scenes, in addition to the statues by the hand of Tribolo.[28]

For her dowry, Eleonora was given 50,000 ducats, which equated to half of what Hürrem received from Süleyman.[29] Before entering Florence, the couple stayed for a while in the villa of Poggio a Caiano, and on 29 June 1539 they made their triumphant entrance into the city.

Like the wedding of Süleyman, Medici's marriage ceremony to Eleonora of Toledo was equally filled with symbolism. Impressive festivities and scenic decorations accompanied the wedding, which was celebrated in San Lorenzo. Accompanying the decorations were various paintings, executed by Battista Franco, Ridolfo del Ghirlandaio and Michele Tosini, that depicted scenes of celebrations and allegories. Performances of Antonio Landi's play, *Il Commodo*, were conducted in the large courtyard of Palazzo Medici and interspersed with intervals that consisted of allegorical scenes by Giovanbattista Strozzi that were set to music by Francesco Corteccia. In addition, the walls were hung with a series of exemplary scenes, featuring illustrious Greeks and Romans on the one hand, and figures from the Medici family on the other, which were painted by Tribolo, Bronzino, Pierfrancesco di Sandro, Francesco Bachiacca, Domenico Conti, Antonio di Domenico, Battista Franco, Francesco Salviati and Carlo Portelli, thereby symbolically connecting the Medici and Renaissance heritage to the classical past. However, the wedding of Süleyman and Hürrem had no need for a triumphal arch, as their backdrop of the ancient Roman Hippodrome is what fused their traditional Ottoman Muslim imperial wedding to the classical past.

Public rituals in Florentine society between the 15th and 16th centuries, according to Testaverde, were fundamental in creating a sense of identity for the community and persuading it to conform to a political programme.[30] In 1588, Bernardo Buontalenti designed sets and costumes in preparation for a performance at the wedding of Grand Duke Ferdinando de' Medici (1549-1609) and Christine of Lorraine. One scene of the performance included characters who were residents of ancient Delphi. However, with their full beards, balloon pants and turbans they looked more like 16th century stereotypical Turks (*Figure 3*). In fact, Buontalenti's conjuring of exotic images from some mythological past demonstrates Ottoman symbolism, and his use of Turkish costumes at the wedding's performance raise questions about the relationship between the Medici and Ottoman court. While the Delphic Turks of Buontalenti's play may have appeared strange at the marriage ceremony, their performance at the *festa* would have enchanted its Florentine audience. Buontalenti's incorporation of exotic costumes, despite the cultural distance between Florence and Istanbul, suggests his play was set in a different time and place.

The impression of Ottoman visual aesthetics as witnessed at the wedding of Süleyman and Hürrem further reinforces Bhaba's assertion of the desire of appropriation rearticulating reality as mimicry.[31] Ironically, it was also an act of integrating Ottoman visual culture into the narrative of Renaissance Italy. The classical allusions combined with the Ottoman visual mode signify a merging of Eastern and Western iconographies. While the fanciful nature of Buontalenti's costume design is obvious, it also points to an aspect of the Grand Duke's personality, who throughout his career held a fascination with Turks and the Islamic world. In fact, he sponsored Arabic press and garden projects, in the Islamic tradition, at his villa in Pratolino.

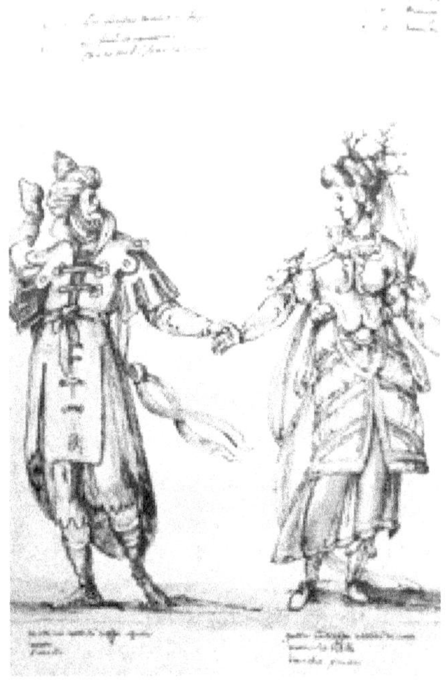

Figure 3. Bernardo Buotalenti, Costume Design for Delphic Couple, 1588, Biblioteca Centrale, Palatina, Florence. Photograph reproduction.

Like Süleyman's majestic ceremonials and pageants, through magnificent spectacles, such as the Grand Duke's wedding, the Medici asserted their princely prominence and erased any trace of their modest origins. As early as 1516, there was growing awareness that the court culture of Florence was changing. Of the courts, Luigi Alamanni observed, "[a]ccustomed as they are to pay respect to none other than their own magistrates and citizens, they show themselves to be alien to court manners in a way I think matched by few others."[32] According to Perkins, these "alien" displays were the results of the following phenomena:

> [S]elf-made signori all over Italy were acutely aware of the questionable nature of their claim to hereditary dominion. For in every aspect of their personal comportment and political activity they

> attempted to convey an impression of the magnificence expected of rulers with their pretensions.[33]

The integration of Ottoman and exotic visual aesthetics with the Medici wedding ceremonies, the Florentines clearly conformed to what the prevalent princely articulation of authority was at the time. Their thirst for luxurious goods and objects from the East reinforces the cross-cultural connections in the early modern Mediterranean. The Ottoman visual mode demonstrates a transformation of Florentine republican iconography, according "to the needs of an emerging and ceremonial court,"[34] which Mulryne explains as:

> [A]n iconography emerged which sought to bring Florence into the mainstream of diplomatic practice alongside comparable city-states, while also flexibly responding to the city's social and political structures which, in contrast to other Italian principates of noble and feudal origin featured an elite of socially privileged and wealthy families no more than reluctantly tolerant of the new court, a process of adjustment which required complex political acculturation.[35]

Furthermore, the dissemination and reception of Ottoman costume books in Europe, by the likes of Lambert de Vos and Sonnegg, provided a means for European engagement with the Orient, and also offer further evidence of the transcultural contact and exchange that occurred during the early modern period.

While the Turks remained a threat to Christendom through the 16th century, they also offered new prototypes of representation that appealed to the Florentines and their celebrations. The pageants and tournaments organised by the Medici, who are traditionally portrayed as classicising humanists, reveal another aspect of their appreciation for the Sultanate ethos that was so brilliantly represented by the Ottoman court. Therefore, like their Ottoman counterparts, "the Medici consciously used symbols to project the desired images of themselves; ... [and support] Savanarola's transformation of carnival behaviour into devout procession."[36] According to Pastore, through their representation of the Ottoman model, Florentines were able to break free from the "ideological and psychological control of ancient and modern Rome."[37] By looking to the East and drawing from Ottoman-Turkish visual tastes, Florentines undermined the Vasarian notion of the *rinascita* or rebirth of classical rediscovery, and therefore, also challenge the 19th century pan-European concept of "the Renaissance," as proposed by Burckhardt and Michelet in the 19th century.

The flexibility of the iconography that was used during the period demonstrates the fluid integration of Ottoman visual motifs; that is, in relation to the distinct idioms of the Renaissance and their allusions to classical symbolism. In fact, without Ottoman-inspired visual cultural influences, the Renaissance narrative, as it is most commonly read, would not have been possible. However, by re-orienting the discourse it is possible to gain a clearer understanding of the early modern period and rely less on a pan-European paradigm.

CREATING THE MYTH OF THE RENAISSANCE CITY: VENICE MEETS OTTOMAN ISTANBUL

Borrowing Burckhardt's title, "The State as a Work of Art" became synonymous with not only 16th century Venice, but also Ottoman Istanbul. The visual imagery and splendour developed by 'la Serenissima Republica,' that is 'the Most Serene Republic of Venice,' as well as Ottoman Istanbul, came to define Renaissance self-fashioning. In the 16th century, these two cities embodied the official iconography of 'the State' and the ways in which they employed this imagery resonated within their respective cultures. There are also parallels between the 'myth' of Venice and the 'myth' of Ottoman Istanbul, in which visual motifs that responded to and manipulated historical events have been used as reliable portraits of each city.

The Myth of Venice

There was a complex interplay of meanings—associated with the Virgin Mary, St. Mark, Wisdom, Justice and Peace—that was central to the popular 'idea' of Venice. According to Rosand, this was no "iconographic slippage," but rather due to active "self-imaging" and a "formal visualization of [a] political ideal ... come to represent the reality of the myth itself."[38] Charles Dempsey shares Rosand's view and delved deeper into the Venetian "myth" that transformed into "reality," as illustrated by the following passage:

> An example is the image of the lion, which taken alone stands for St. Mark, the city's patron and so can also stand for Venice itself. In the biblical book of Wisdom, Divine Wisdom is personified seated on the lion-throne of Solomon, and lions flanking a throne thus signify her ... Biblical exegesis equates Divine Wisdom and the Virgin, and Jacobello depicted the Archangel Gabriel with Madonna lilies and a scroll to the right of Justice (who is crowned like the Queen of Heaven ... This inevitably evokes Venice's other patron, for the city has been founded on the feast of the Annunciation ... the concepts of Justice founded in Divine Wisdom, the Virgin, St. Mark, and of course Venice herself, are seamlessly joined.[39]

Here, religious allusions to biblical prophets served to forge the myth of the city of Venice and became a catalyst for its early modern identity formation.

Whether Venice was personified in paintings, such as Veronese's *Apotheosis of Venice* (1585), or represented as Venus, whose beauty was born of the sea, the iconographic metonyms of such myths presented the city and its ceremonies, but also magnified the image of Venice. For example, in *Apotheosis of Venice*, her personified figure is shown dressed in royal dress and enthroned between the twin towers of the city's Arsenal.[40] She is about to be crowned by flying victories, who carry her laurel crown, and at her feet—offering wise counsel—are according to Paoletti and Radke, "... personifications of Peace, Abundance, Fame, Happiness, Honour, Security and Freedom."[41] A triumphal arch with "twisted columns" marks the top of an immense balcony, which seems to "burst through the ceiling and into the ether beyond" [42]—apparently, as stipulated in the commission of the work, in order to accommodate for multitudes of celebrating onlookers. At the base of the painting, Venice's cheerful subjects seem undisturbed by the enormity of the traversing horsemen in their midst, who act as reminders of the military power of Venice.[43] Paoletti and Radke informs the illusionistic portrayals and dramatic light effects in the painting are intended to produce "political allegory"[44] of the rebirth of Venice as a dynamic Mediterranean thalassocracy challenging its Muslim 'Other,' the Ottomans, in the centuries to come (*Figure 4*).

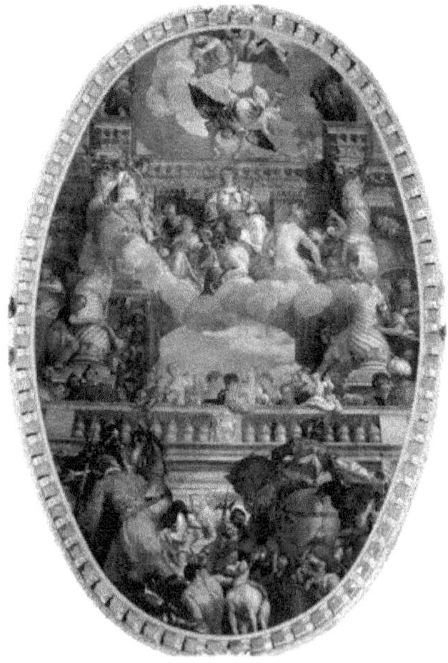

Figure 4. Paolo Veronese, The Apotheosis of Venice, 1585, Hall of the Senate, Palazzo Ducale, Venice. Photograph reproduction.

Ottoman Renaissance objects serve as decorative ornaments in paintings. The paintings of Gentile Bellini's 1496 painting of the *Procession in the Piazza San Marco,* which was commissioned by the Scuola Grande di S. Giovanni Evangelista, depicts an annual event that is held on 25 April to celebrate the feast day of St. Mark; in honour of the working miracle of the relic of the True Cross. In the painting, the confraternity can be seen marching through the piazza, preceded by a choir and honour guard of marchers holding large candlesticks (called *doppieri*) surrounded by Turkish-inspired Hans Holbein carpets hanging from the balconies of St. Mark's Square. The relic of the True Cross sits under a fabric cover and is carried on a decorated platform. However, the painting also demonstrates the civic values of Venice, which are represented in features such as a canopy that is decorated with the coats of arms of all the *scuole grandi*. Additionally, the painting includes Venetians from all walks of life; whether secular or religious, its citizens are shown as lines of spectators who fill the piazza and windows of the palaces, as seen on the right side. On the far right of the painting, the Doge is also visible, but preceded by groups of standard bearers and trumpeters, followed by patrician magistrates and high-ranking officials. The particular order used within the procession aligns with Venetian rankings of caste, office and seniority, and underscores the city's stability (*Figure 5*).

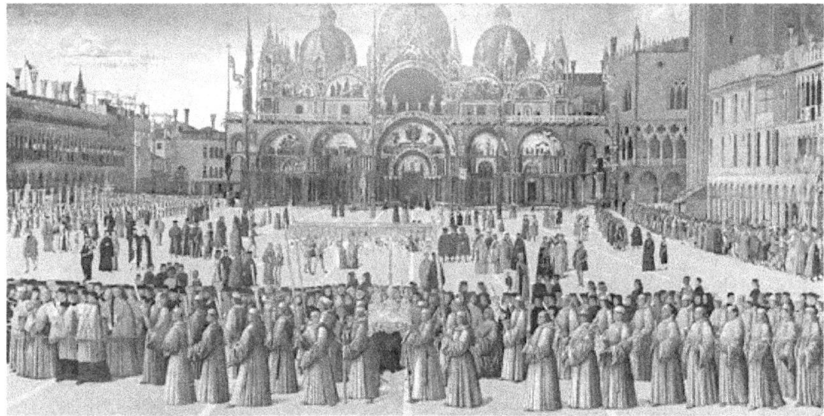

Figure 5. Gentile Bellini's political depiction of the Procession in the Piazza San Marco (1496). Photograph reproduction.

Venetian sculptural embellishments equally contributed to the iconography of the 'myth' of Venice. As observed earlier, Venice came to embody Justice and that virtue emanates through the Ducal Palace of the Doge. "The meaning of the Ducal Palace," according to Rosand, "was quite clear: as Venice herself was equated with Justice, so the palace of the doge was to be considered a palace of Solomon—"[45] the Old Testament patriarch who constructed the House of God and the house of the king. For example, the palace constructed under Doge Francesco Foscari (1423-57)—at its corner "adjacent to the Porta della Carta, above the capital of the massive column, a sculpted group representing the Judgment of Solomon announces the major theme of the Ducal Palace in a narrative key."[46] As its central motif, to represent scenes of justice and dispensers of law, on the capital below are the figures of Aristotle, Moses, Solon, Scipio, Numa Pompilius and Trajan —all personifying Justice.[47] The legibility of such imagery did not miss the Florentine visitor in 1442 describing the palace in verse: "In which is seen the memory / Of wise Solomon with the justice / He rendered to those women."[48] In other words, Venetians required narratives to visually reinforce and confirm the political, economic, and social strength and authority of the Serenissima (i.e. Venice). Furthermore, Venice sought to solidify its position as the true successor of the ancient Roman Republic—on which it modelled its system of government.

The Myth of Ottoman Istanbul

The Ottoman myth about the city of Istanbul was based on the religious iconography of the Holy Mantle, Holy Standard and burial shrine of Ayyub (Eyüp in Turkish)—the Prophet's companion who died at the Arab siege of Constantinople in the seventh century. Such a myth was created for reasons similar to the Venetian's regarding their stories about Venice. The lack of an Ottoman bloodline that could directly connect it to Islam created conflict in the minds of many Ottomans. Even a 16th century Grand Vizier, Lutfi Pasha, questioned how an Ottoman Sultan could be the 'Shadow of God' when he could not claim direct ancestry to the Prophet or his family.[49] Therefore, in place of a bloodline, the Holy Mantle and caliphate became symbolic of the House of Osman, and through ceremonial rituals the sacred city and the Sultan's residence—*Der'i Sa'adet* (House of Good Fortune)—were used to construct the Ottoman myth. Like the Venetians, the Ottomans used religious rituals to establish unity and order in the city, and most importantly, to legitimise and amplify their Islamic prestige as caliphs in the Muslim world.

Of the three religious rituals, the first was the ceremony for the Sultan and his court, which occurred within the palace during the month of Ramadan. Süleyman's father Selim I originally brought the Prophet's Mantle and other relics of Muhammad to Istanbul after his conquest of Egypt, Mecca and Medina in 1516-17. Officials, scholars, pashas, viziers, the Grand Vizier and the Şeyhülislam (the Empire's leading religious authority) had new clothing prepared to wear for the event. However, no medallions or jewellery of any kind were permitted because such adornments may have caught on the cover of the Mantle as they leaned over it to kiss it.

On the fourteenth day of Ramadan, the Holy Mantle would be transferred to the Revan Pavilion of the Palace. Prior to this, the Sultan, viziers and other officials would use a symbolic gesture to sweep the chamber clean and signify their servitude to the Prophet, which they regarded as a great honour. Additionally, the walls would be washed with rose water and perfumed with musk, which symbolised the scent of Paradise. On the fifteenth day, all the officials, scholars, janissaries and cavalry officers would gather during noon prayer time at the Palace's Gate of Felicity and wait for the Grand Vizier while the *Şeyhülislam* (chief Islamic cleric of the Empire) led the congregation in prayer at the Hagia Sophia. After prayers, the group proceeded to the chamber according to rank—i.e. the Sultan followed by the *Şeyhülislam* and Grand Vizier, who were followed by scholars, state officials of Istanbul, the Head of the Janissaries and Cavalry, the Sword Bearer, the Head Footman, the Head Equerry, the Chief Servant of the Table for Handkerchiefs and the Head Servant of the Keys—to view and kiss the Holy Mantle while the Qur'an was recited in the background.

The Sultan would then send peace and blessings to the Prophet. Bringing a large golden basin to the visitors' space filled with *zamzam* holy water from Mecca, the edges of the Prophet's Mantle would be lightly dipped in it. The holy water from Mecca signifies the link to Abraham, Hagar and Ishmael, who was saved by the *zamzam* water in the desert after Patriarch Abraham left them there.[50] This ritual symbolically connects the Ottoman Sultan-Caliphate not only to the Prophet through his holy Mantle, but to Abraham as well, considered to be the "father of many nations," thereby creating a sacrosanct image of the Sultan before the eyes of his multi-ethnic, multi-lingual, and multi-religious subjects (i.e. his *millets*), and thus solidifying his Caliph status even further (*Figure 6*).[51]

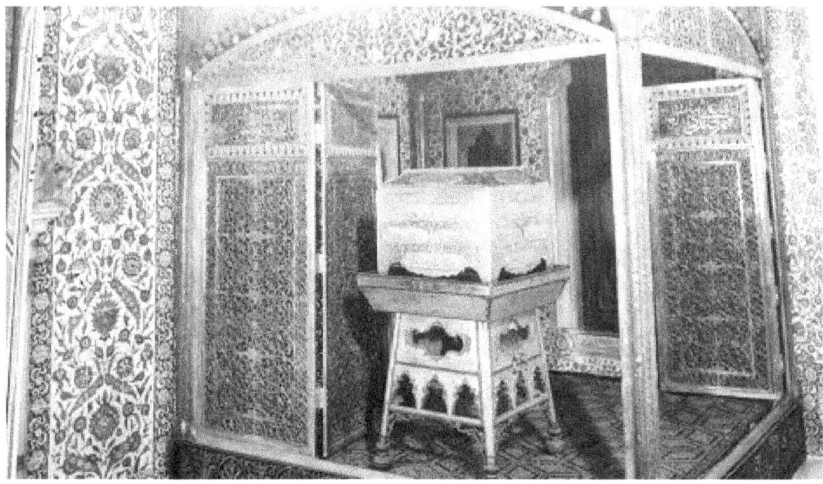

Figure 6. The Room of the Holy Mantle, Topkapı Palace, Istanbul. Photograph by Metin Mustafa, December 2014.

The second religious ritual was tied not only to military campaigns, but also the notion (and myth) of the holiness of the city. The Procession of the Honoured Standard of the Prophet would be raised on a flagpole 40 days before the Sultan embarked on his military campaign (*Figure 7-8*). The remains of the Prophet's fragile flag were appropriated by Ottoman artists who recreated it with red and green Bursa silk and the names of the Prophet's ten companions, which were embroidered, in silver thread, on the red section of the flag. This ceremony held a special significance for the people of Istanbul, and according to

Hilmi Aydın, "they filled the streets from Ayasofya square to Edirnekapı, and from there to Davutpaşa. As depicted in the miniature painting to see the [Holy Mantle and] Honoured Standard was considered a meritorious act, as well as means of hope for the ill, young children, and those in difficulty"[52] (*Figure 9*).

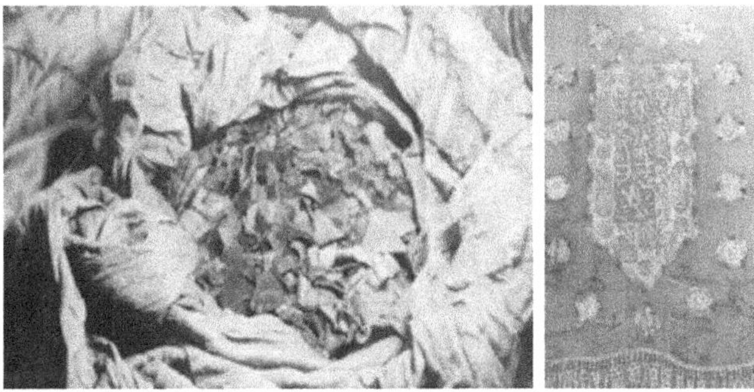

Figures 7 and 8. The black flag of the Honoured Standard "Uqab," which belonged to the Prophet is kept in green silk bag. It disintegrated over the centuries, Topkapı Palace Museum. The Honoured Standard was remade by the Ottomans with pieces of the original flag sewn on with verses from the Qur'an and the names of the ten companions of the Prophet, Topkapı Palace Museum. Photograph reproductions.

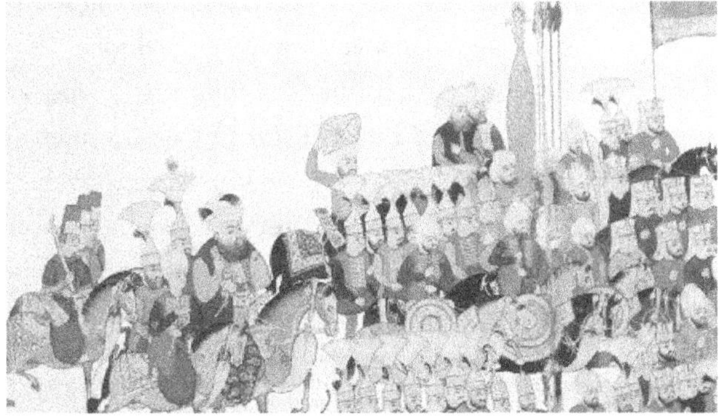

Figure 9. Parading the Holy Mantle and Honoured Standard. Miniature painting, Topkapı Palace Museum, Istanbul. Photograph reproduction.

Being in possession of such holy objects allowed the Sultan-Caliphate to legitimise its authority to rule over the Islamic world and, therefore, set its visual discourse on an aesthetic path that followed its cultural traditions. However, while their aesthetics differed from their Renaissance counterparts, their purpose did not.

Third, with the burial place of the Prophet's companion, Ayyub, located in Istanbul, the Ottoman myth became a reality for the sultanate. The founding of his remains by Mehmed II's spiritual Sufi, Sheykh Akshemseddin—before the conquest of the city in 1453—and the mosque that was built at the site by the Conqueror, represented spiritual significance and Islamic legitimacy for the Ottoman Turks, in addition to Prophet Muhammad's prophecy that a Muslim army would conquer Constantinople.[53] These factors combined to create a link between the new capital and the Prophet. Additionally, 'Ayyub' became 'Eyüp' in Turkish, and the patron saint of Ottoman Istanbul. By the middle of the 16th century the Mosque of Eyüp became a pilgrimage centre for Muslims and took the title of 'fourth most holy site'—after Mecca, Medina and Jerusalem. It also became the coronation mosque for Ottoman sultans where they were girded with the sword of Osman, the founder of the dynasty. According to Colin Imber,

---

> Selim [II] had set a precedent, and all future sultans followed him in making the pilgrimage soon after coming to the throne. The fact, however, that Murad III delayed the occasion for two weeks after his accession in 1574 and Mehmed III for five weeks after his in 1595 suggests that it was not yet a firmly established ritual [...] but it was Ahmed I's accession that the ceremony took its final form. When he had arrived at the mausoleum and prayed to the saint, the chief mufti girded him with a 'victory-bringing sword'.[54]

The coronation ceremony at the Mosque of Eyüp reflected the Ottoman myth as reality. Not only was it a display of a symbolic connection to the Prophet, it also represented the Ottomans' militaristic zeal, as signified by the "victory-bringing sword" with which the sultan would expand his realm. By possessing the relics of the Prophet and housing them at the sultan's palace or the annual court, and using them in religious ceremonies, such as those associated with the Mosque of Eyüp, the allegory of 'Holy' Istanbul and the legitimate Ottoman Caliphate-Sultanate were symbolically solidified. Like Venice, the Ottoman elite deemed it necessary to forge an identity through myth to legitimise its imperial presence and provide the former Eastern Roman capital, Constantinople, a new Islamic character – Ottoman Istanbul.

CONCLUSION

Early modern festivities, weddings and pageantries represent the celebration of Renaissance material culture. Equally, they represent a search for court identity and legitimacy. According to Loren Partridge and Randolf Starn, the "art making" and other propagandistic displays of the emerging early modern societies, were "product[s] of the triumphalist state. It involved a large bureaucracy, an extensive division of labour, a careful allocation of resources, all controlled from the top to mobilize the display of intellectual, artistic, and material resources."[55] Based on Partridge and Starn's view, it was clearly an experience that occurred in the Ottoman Empire of the Süleymanic Age and Renaissance Europe. Another significant point about the iconography of these events is they represented a hybrid art form that fused instrumental music, song, dance, and lavish costumes and stage designs to glorify the ruling elite. It was not only the ruling elite of Renaissance Italy who took centre stage, but also the visual culture of the Ottoman court. Thierry Hentsch describes the phenomenon as:

[The] Orient was not simply a mirror, but the indispensable complement of a Western civilisation which searched for totality and plenitude in fusion with it, sought coherence continuity in a philosophy of history which saw pre-Hellenic antiquity conscripted into the service of European [Renaissance] universalism.[56]

Historically speaking, the cultural rebirth through *imitazione* (imitation) and *adeguazione* (adaptation) noted by Vasari and concurred by Bhabha, demonstrate a convergence of the Renaissance paradigm, one that includes similar visual practices from different cultural traditions rather than excludes. It was through the visual and material fusion of the Ottoman world with Renaissance representations of political entities that discourses became intertwined and converged. Such a view also suggests Renaissance Italy consciously accepted its classical heritage and equally, its indebtedness to the Ottoman Renaissance legacy that enriched its being.

Bibliography

Alberi, Eugino. *Le Relazioni Degli Ambasciatori Veneti*. Firenze: A Spese

Dell'Editore, 1863. Accessed June 14, 2015. https://archive.org/stream/E.AlberiRelazioniDegliAmbasciatori-Veneti-Serie3-Vol.1/Alberi.Vol.I_djvu.txt.

Aydın, H. *Pavilion of the Sacred Relics: The Sacred Trusts, Topkapi Palace Museum*. Istanbul, Clifton, USA: Tughra Books, 2011.

Bhabha, Homi K. *The Location of Culture.* New York: Routledge, 2004. Kindle Edition.

Brotton, Jerry. *The Renaissance: A Very Short Introduction.* New York: Oxford University Press, 2006.

Burioni, Matteo. Vasari's Rinascita: History, Anthropology or Art Criticism. Leiden, The Netherlands: Koninklijke Brill NV, 2010. Accessed March 14, 2014. https://www.academia.edu/2638258/Vasari_s_rinascita._History_anthropology_or_art_criticism

La Corte, il Mare, i Mercanti. Firenze: Electa, 1980.

Dimashqi, Ibn Katheer. *Book of the End: Great Trials and Tribulations*. Translated by Faisal Shafiq. Riyadh: Darussalam, 2006.

Hentsch, Thierry. *Imagining the Middle East.* Montreal: Black Rose Books, 1992.

Imber, Colin. *The Ottoman Empire, 1300-1650: The Structure of Power.* New York: Palgrave Macmillan, 2002.

Inalcık, Halil. *The Middle East and the Balkans under the Ottoman Empire.* Bloomington: Indiana University Turkish Studies Department, 1993.

Khan, Muhsin, trans. *The Translation of the Meanings of Summarized Sahih-Al-Bukhari: Arabic-English*. Lahore: Kazi Publications Inc., 1995.

Machiavelli, Niccolò. "Discourses on Livy." In *The Prince and the Discourses*, edited and translated by Luigi Ricci, 103-538. New York: Modern Library, 1950.

Mansel, Philip. *Constantinople: City of the World's Desire, 1453-1924.* London, UK: John Murray, 1995.

Menemencioğlu, N., ed. *The Penguin Verse of Turkish Verse*. Suffolk, UK: Penguin Books Ltd., 1978.

Mulryne, J. R., Maria Ines Aliverti and Anna Maria Testaverde, eds. *Ceremonial Entries in Early Modern Europe: The Iconography of Power.* England: Ashgate, 2015.

Necipoğlu, Gülru. "Süleyman the Magnificent and Representations of Power in the Context of Ottoman-Habsburg Papal Rivalry." *The Art Bulletin* 71, no. 3 (1989): 401-427. Accessed August 3, 2014. http://www.jstor.org/stable/3051136.

Olian, Joanne. "Sixteenth Century Books." *Costume* 3 (1977): 20-48.

Paoletti, J., and G. M. Radke, *Art in Renaissance Italy*. London: Laurence King Publishing, 2005.

Partridge, Lauren, and Randolf Starn. *Arts of Power: Three Halls of State in Italy, 1300-1600.* Berkeley and Los Angeles: University of California Press, 1992.

Pastore, C. "Bipolar Behavior: Ferdinando I de' Medici and the East." In *The Turk and Islam in the Western Eye, 1450-1750: Visual Imagery before Orientalism*, edited by J. G. Harper, 129-154. New York: Taylor & Francis, 2011.

Peirce, Leslie P. *The Imperial Harem: Women and Sovereignty in the Ottoman Empire*. New York: Oxford University Press, 1993.

Perkins, L. L. *Music in the Age of the Renaissance*. New York: W. W. Norton & Company, 1999.

Rosand, David. *Myths of Venice: The Figuration of a State.* Library of Congress, Washington DC: University of North Carolina Press, 2001.

Rosand, David. "Myths of Venice: The Figuration of a State." *Renaissance Quarterly* 56, no. 2 (2003): 454-456. Accessed July 15, 2014. http://www.jstor.org/stable/1261857.

Said, Edward. *Orientalism*. London, UK: Penguin Books, 1995.

Saslow, J. M. *Florentine Festival as 'Theatrum Mundi': The Medici Wedding of 1589*. New Haven and London: Yale University Press, 1996.

Selaniki, Mustafa Efendi. *Tarih-i Selaniki*, vol. 1. Edited by Mehmet Ispirli. Istanbul: Türk Tarih Kurum Basımevi, 1989.

Taylor, T. D. *Beyond Exoticism. Western Music and the World*. Durham and London: Duke University Press, 2007.

Terzioğlu, Deniz. "The Imperial Circumcision Festival of 1582: An Interpretation." *Muqarnas* 12 (1995): 84-100.

Testaverde, Anna Maria. "The Book of Ceremonies of Francesco Tongiarini (1536-1612)." In *Ceremonial Entries in Early Modern Europe: The Iconography of Power*, edited by J. R. Mulryne, Maria Ines Aliverti and Anna Maria Testaverde, 99-112.England: Ashgate, 2015.

Tinagli, P. *Women in Italian Renaissance Art: Gender, Representation and Identity*. New York: Manchester University Press, 1997.

Trexler, R. C. *Public Life in Florence*. London: Cornell University Press, 1980.

Vasari, Giorgio. *Vasari's Lives of the Artists*. Translated by Jonathan Foster. New York: Dover Publications, 2005. Kindle edition.

Yerasimos, Stephane. "The Imperial Procession: Recreating a World's Order." In *Surname-I Vehbi*. Accessed September 23, 2014. http://web.archive.org/web/20091025054327/http://geocities.com/surnamei_vehbi/yerasimos.html.

Young, George. *Constantinople.* New York: Dorset House Publishing Co Inc., 1997.

Notes

UNDERSTANDING "ZEITGEIST"

1. Monika Krause, 'What is Zeitgeist? Examining period-specific cultural patterns,' Department of Sociology, London School of Economics, 2016, accessed February 3, 2021, http://eprints.lse.ac.uk/100076/3/1_s2.0_S0304422X18301931_main.pdf
2. K. Mannheim, *Essays on the Sociology of Knowledge* (London: Routledge, 1952).
3. Warwick Ball, *Sultans of Rome: The Turkish World Expansion* (Northhampton, MA: Olive Branch Press, 2013), 23.
4. Krause, 'What is Zeitgeist?
5. Mannheim, *Essyas on the Sociology of Knowledge*, 6.
6. For more see H. Focillon, *The life of forms in art* (New York: Zone Books, 1989).
7. For more see G. W. F. Hegel, *Lectures on the Philosophy of History*, trans., J. Sibree (London: George Bell and Sons, 1902); also see John Shannon Hendrix, *Aesthetics & The Philosophy Of Spirit* (New York: Peter Lang. (2005), 4, 11.

1. THE RENAISSANCE PARADIGM: A REVISIONIST PERSPECTIVE

1. For an extensive analysis of this work see Metin Mustafa, *The Ottoman Renaissance: A Reconsideration of Early Modern Ottoman Art, 1413-1575* (New Jersey: Blue Dome Press, 2019); also see Metin Mustafa, *History of Ottoman Renaissance Art: From Mehmed I to Selim II* (Sydney: Centre for Ottoman Renaissance and Civilisation, 2020). Revised Edition.
2. The essay will refer to both electronic and hard copy publications of the text of Giorgio Vasari. Giorgio Vasari, *The Lives of the Painters, Sculptors and Architects*, accessed May 5, 2016, http://members.efn.org/~acd/vite/VasariLives.html; Giorgio Vasari, *The Lives of the Painters, Sculptors and Architects*, translated by Jonathan Foster (New York: Dover Publications, 2005), Kindle edition; for book publication, Giorgio Vasari, *The Lives of the Painters, Sculptors and Architects*, 4 vols., edited by William Gaunt (New York: Dent, 1963).
3. For more see E. H. Gombrich, 'The Renaissance Conception of Artistic Progress and its Consequences', in *Norm and Form: Studies in the Art of the Renaissance* (London: Phaidon Press, 1966), 1-10.
4. '…della loro perfezione e rovina e restaurazione e per dir meglio rinascita…', Giorgio Vasari, Le vite de' piu eccellenti pittori, scultori ed architetti (Torino: Letteratura italiana Einaudi, 1986), 125, http://www.letteraturaitaliana.net/pdf/Volume_5/t129.pdf. For English translation see Vasari, Preface to Part I, *The Lives*, accessed May 5, 2016, http://members.efn.org/~acd/vite/VasariPreface.html
5. Vasari, Preface to Part II, *The Lives*, accessed May 5, 2016, http://members.efn.org/~acd/vite/VasariPreface2.html
6. Vasari, Part III of *The Lives*.

7. For more see Hans Baron, *The Crisis of the Early Italian Renaissance* (Princeton: Princeton University Press, 1966).
8. Vasari, Preface to *The Lives.*
9. '...lavorata di mano d'Andrea Taffi con la medesima maniera greca, ma invero molto piú bella ...' Giorgio Vasari, *Le vite de' piu eccellenti architetti pittori, et scultori italiani da Cimabue insino a'tempi nostri* (Firenze: Torentino, 1550), http://bepi1949.altervista.org/vasari/vasari10.htm
10. Vasari, Part I of *The Lives,* accessed May 5, 2016, http://members.efn.org/~acd/vite/VasariGioPisano.html
11. Vasari, Part I of *The Lives,* http://members.efn.org/~acd/vite/VasariGioPisano.html
12. Vasari, Part III of *The Lives,* accessed May 5, 2016, http://members.efn.org/~acd/vite/VasariMichelangelo7.html
13. Lee Sanstead, 'The Meaning of Michelangelo's David' (5 September 2004), accessed February 19, 2017, http://www.sandstead.com/essays/david.html
14. Vasari, Part III of *The Lives,* http://members.efn.org/~acd/vite/VasariMichelangelo3.html
15. Vasari, Part III of *The Lives,* http://members.efn.org/~acd/vite/VasariMichelangelo3.html
16. Vasari, Preface to *The Lives.*
17. Ulrich Libbrecht, 'Comparative Philosophy: A Methodological Approach,' in *Worldviews and Cultures: Philosophical Reflections from an Intercultural Perspective,* edited by Nicole Note et al., (Brussels: Springer, 2009), 34.
18. Vasari, Preface to *The Lives.*
19. Vasari, Preface to *The Lives.*
20. Also see Alexander Nagel and Christopher Wood, 'Towards a New Model of Renaissance Anachronism,' *Art Bulletin* 87 (2005): 408.
21. Walter B. Denny, *Iznik: The Artistry of Ottoman Ceramics* (London: Thames and London, reprinted 2010), 18.
22. Leibniz in T. Hentsch, *Imagining the Middle East* (Montreal: Black Rose Books, 1992), 96.
23. James R. Lehning, *To be a Citizen: The Political Culture of the Early French Third Republic* (London: Cornell University Press, 2001), 132.
24. For more see P. Murray and L. Murray, *The Art of the Renaissance* (London, Thames and London) 1963, 9; Brotton, *The Renaissance Bazaar,* Kindle edition, 21–22; also see Jacob Burckhardt, *The Civilisation of the Renaissance in Italy* (Pisa: Aonia edizioni, 2011).
25. Michelet, cited in Brotton, *The Renaissance Bazaar,* Loc.254.
26. Michelet, cited in Brotton, *The Renaissance Bazaar,* Loc.260.
27. Burckhardt, *The Civilisation of the Renaissance in Italy,* 9.
28. W. K. Ferguson, *The Renaissance in Historical Thought* (Cambridge, MA: Houghton Mifflin Company, 1948), 222-223, 240-243.
29. Ferguson, *The Renaissance in Historical Thought,* 28; M. L. McLaughlin, 'Humanist Concept of Renaissance and Middle Ages in the Tre- and Quattrocento,' *Renaissance Studies* 2 (1988): ix, 131-42.
30. For more see Arthur Hughes, 'Interpreting the Renaissance,' *Oxford Art Journal* 11 (1988): 77-78.
31. Edward Said, *Orientalism* (London: Penguin Books, 1995), 7.
32. Erwin Panofsky, *Renaissance and Renascences in Western Art* (Almqvist & Wiksell, 1969), 38.

33. Brotton, *The Renaissance Bazaar,* Loc. 364.
34. Said, *Orientalism,* 342-343.
35. Z. Sardar, *Orientalism* (Buckingham: Open University Press, 1999), vii.
36. Sardar, *Orientalism,* 31.
37. Claire Norton, 'Blurring the Boundaries: Intellectual and Cultural Interactions between Eastern and Western: Christian and Muslim Worlds', in *The Renaissance and the Ottoman World,* edited by Anna Contadini and Claire Norton (England: Ashgate Publishing Limited, 2013), 3.
38. See Homi Bhabha, *The Location of Cultures* (London & New York: Routledge, 1994), Kindle edition.
39. Stuart Hill, 'The Spectacle of the 'Other'', in *Representation: Cultural Representations and Signifying Practices,* edited by Stuart Hill (London: Sage Publications, 2003), 261.
40. Hill, 'The Spectacle of the 'Other'', 271.
41. MacClean, 'Introduction: Re-Orienting the Renaissance', in *Re-Orienting the Renaissance,* 8. For more on revisionist historiography see D. J. Castellano's essay on 'The Renaissance Concept of Self as seen in Petrarch, Castiglione and Montaigne,' (Massachusetts: Boston University, 2002), accessed May 23, 2016, http://www.arcane-knowledge.org/histschol/renaissance.htm
42. Jardine and Brotton, *Global Interest,* 61.
43. Jardine and Brotton, *Global Interest,* 61.
44. Jardine and Brotton, *Global Interest,* 61.
45. Jardine, *Worldly Goods,* back cover.
46. Jardine, *Worldly Goods,* xi.
47. See Brotton, *The Renaissance: A Very Short Introduction,* 8; also see Matteo Burioni, 'Vasari's Rinascita: History, Anthropology or Art Criticism,' accessed January 29, 2016, https://www.academia.edu/2638258/Vasari_s_rinascita._History_anthropology_or_art_criticis, 117.
48. Mack, *Bazaar to Piazza,* 179.
49. Friedrich Adler, 'Die Moscheen zu Constantinopel: Eine architektonische baugeschictliche Studie,' (The Mosques of Constantinople: An Architectural Study), *Deutsche Bauzeitung* 8 (1874): 65–66, 73–76, 81–83, 89–91, 97– 99.
50. See Corneilus Gurlitt, *Istanbul'un Mimari Sanatı, Architecture of Constantinople, Die Baukunst Konstantinopels* translated by Rezan Kæzæltan (Ankara: Enformasyon ve Dokumantasyon Hizmetleri Vakfı, 1999), 59, 66, 96. The work has been translated from Cornelius Gurlitt, *Die Baukunst Konstantinopels,* 2 vols. (Berlin: 1907).
51. Gurlitt, *Istanbul'un Mimari Sanatı.*
52. See Franz Babinger, 'Die türkische Renaissance: Bemerkungen zum Schaffen des grossen türkischen Baumeisters Sinân,' *Beiträge zur Kenntnis des Orients* 9 (1914): 67–88.
53. Franz Babinger, 'Ein osmanischer Michelangelo,' *Frankfurter Zeitung,* Sept. 7, 1915, no. 248.
54. Ernst Diez, *Türk Sanatı: Başlangıcından Günümüze Kadar,* trans. Oktay Aslanapa, (Istanbul, 1946), 232.
55. Diez, *Türk Sanatı,* 232.
56. Diez, *Türk Sanatı,* 6 7, 27, 138–39, 170, 192–98 Also see Halil Inalcık, *The Ottoman Empire: The Classical Age 1300–1600,* (London: Butler & Tanner, 1973).
57. Esin Atıl, *Süleymanname: The Illustrated History of Süleyman the Magnificent* (Washington: National Gallery of Art, 1986), 31. Also see *The Age of Süleyman the Magnificent,* (NSW, Australia: Art Exhibitions Australia / Beagle Press, 1990, Exhibition Publication); Esin Atıl, 'The Image of Süleyman in Ottoman Art,' in *Süleyman the Second and*

His Time, edited by Halil Inalcik and Cemal Kafadar (Istanbul: The Isis Press, 2010), 333–341.

58. Doğan Kuban, *Ottoman Architecture* (Suffolk, UK: Antique Collectors Club Distributors, 2010), 246-247.
59. 'Interview with Gülru Necipoğlu,' by Gizem Tongo, Department of History at Bogaziçi University, Istanbul, August 2009, accessed, August 15, 2017, http://isites.harvard.edu/fs/docs/icb.topic732589.files//Gizem_Tongo_Interview-GULRU_NECIPOGLU.pdf
60. Godfrey Goodwin, *A History of Ottoman Architecture* (London, UK: Thames and Hudson, 1971), 6.
61. Denny, *Iznik: The Artistry of Ottoman Ceramics*, 22.
62. See Nurhan Atasoy and Julian Raby. *Iznik: The Pottery of Ottoman Turkey*, edited by Yanni Petsopoulos (London: Thames and Hudson, 1989), 14-49; also see Atıl, *Süleymanname*, 31-35.
63. Bisaha, *Creating East and West*, 174.
64. Bisaha, *Creating East and West*, 174.
65. James Hankins, 'Renaissance Crusaders: Humanist Crusade Literature in the Age of Mehmed II,' in *Dumbarton Oaks Papers*, Vol. 49, Symposium on Byzantium and the Italians, 13th-15th Centuries (1995): 111-207. Also see Hentsch, *Imagining the Middle East*, 165; Paul Coles, *Ottoman Impact on Europe* (Harcourt: Brace & World, 1968), 12; Bernard Lewis, *Islam and the West* (London: Oxford University Press, 1993).
66. S. Yerasimos, *Constantinople: Istanbul's Historical Heritage* (Paris: H. F. Ullmann Publishing, 2012), 276. Also see Henry Matthews, 'Rethinking Ottoman Architecture.' Paper presented at the ACSA International Conference, 2001; Brian Sewell, 'Sinan: The Architect of a Forgotten Renaissance,' *Cornucopia*, 1992/93.
67. Selda Besnier- Kılıçioğlu, 'Sinan and Palladio: The Parallel Development of Two Master-Builders,' *The UNESCO Courier: a window open on the world* XLI, no. 3 (1988), accessed March 4, 2014, http://unesdoc.unesco.org/images/0007/000781/078126eo.pdf#77905, p.34.
68. Ruggiero, *A Companion to the Worlds of the Renaissance*, 3.
69. Colin H. Fleischer, *Bureaucrat and Intellectual in the Ottoman Empire: The Historian Mustafa Ali, 1541-1600* (Princeton: Princeton University Press, 1986), 274.
70. Giorgio Vasari, *Vasari's Lives of the Artists*, translated by Jonathan Foster (New York: Dover Publications, 2005), Kindle edition, Loc.29.
71. Vasari, *Vasari's Lives of the Artists*, Kindle edition, Loc.28.
72. Fleischer, *Bureaucrat and Intellectual in the Ottoman Empire*, 123.
73. Akın's commentary in Mustafa Ali, *Epic Deeds of Artists: A Critical Edition of the Earliest Ottoman Text about the Calligraphers and Painters of the Islamic World*, edited, translated and commented by Esra Akın-Kıvanç (Leiden: Brill, 2011), 118, 378. Translation of 'silsile-i celileye ihtisasla': reaching state of specialisation in one's craft from one era to the next.
74. Esin Atıl, *Süleymanname: The Illustrated History of Süleyman the Magnificent* (Washington: National Gallery of Art, 1986), 32-49.
75. See Ali, *Epic Deeds of Artists*, 273.
76. Ali, cited in Fleischer, *Bureaucrat and Intellectual in the Ottoman Empire*, 278.
77. Ali, *Epic Deeds of Artists*, 147.
78. Ali, *Epic Deeds of Artists*, 273.
79. Ali, *Epic Deeds of Artists*, 198.
80. Ali, *Epic Deeds of Artists*, 410, 417. For Ottoman-Turkish definitions see Ottoman-Turkish Dictionary, *Yeni Cep Lügat* (Istanbul: Envar Neşriyat, 2000).

81. Ali, *Epic Deeds of Artists*, 174.
82. Ali, *Epic Deeds of Artists*, 319.
83. Ali, *Epic Deeds of Artists*, 313.
84. Ali, *Epic Deeds of Artists*, 196.
85. Ali, *Epic Deeds of Artists*, 196.
86. Ali, *Epic Deeds of Artists*, 294, 330, 334, 384.
87. J. M. Rogers and R. M. Ward, *Süleyman the Magnificent* (London: British Museum Publications, 1990), 55.
88. Ali mentions the original 'six styles' of Arabic as *thuluth, naskh, tafiliq, rayhani, muhaqqaq*, and *riqa*.
89. Ali, *Epic Deeds of Artists*, 147.
90. Ali, *Epic Deeds of Artists*, 202.
91. Mustafa Sa'i, *Sinan's Autobiographies: Five Sixteenth Century Texts, Introductory Notes, Critical Editions, and Translations by Howard Crane and Esra Akın*, edited by Gülru Necipoğlu (Leiden: Brill, 2006), 124.
92. Ali, *Epic Deeds of Artists*, 454.
93. Ali, *Epic Deeds of Artists*, 273.
94. Ali, *Epic Deeds of Artists*, 273. According to Maria Pia Pedani, Paoli might be the Maestro Paolo of Ragusa, Sicily. The author shows that in 1480 Sinan Bey was sent to Venice as an envoy. Esin Atıl includes a list of other Italian painters who worked at Topkapı Palace: Bartholomeo di San Marco, Gentile Bellini, Costanzo da Ferrara, Matteo de Pasti, Paolo da Pistoja, Paolo da Ragusa, Paolo Uccello, and Pinturicchio. See Esin Atıl, 'Ottoman Miniature Painting Under Sultan Mehmed II,' *Ars Oreintalis V*, IX, (1973): 103-120.
95. Also known as Ahmed of Bursa, another Ottoman artist who painted Sultan Mehmed II, in his portrait Mehmed II Smelling a Rose. See Gülru Necipoğlu, 'From Byzantine Constantinople to Ottoman Konstantiniyye: Creation of a Cosmopolitan Capital and Visual Culture Under Sultan Mehmed II,' in *From Byzantium to Istanbul: 8000 Years of Capital*, edited by Nazan Ölçer (Istanbul: Sabanci University, Sakip Sabanci Museum, 2010), 265-276.
96. Necipoğlu, 'From Byzantine Constantinople to Ottoman Konstantiniyye,' 274.
97. See Hans Georg Majer, 'New Approaches in Portraiture,' in *The Sultan's Portrait: Picturing the House of Osman*, ed. Selmin Kangal (Istanbul: İşBank, 2000), 336–375, 344; also see Gülru Necipoğlu, 'The Serial Portraits of Ottoman Sultans in Comparative Perspective,' in *The Sultan's Portrait: Picturing the House of Osman*, ed. Selmin Kangal and trans. Priscilla Mary Işın (Istanbul: İşBank, 2000), 37; Robin Beuchat, 'Échange interculturel et transfert de representations Sur les portraits turcs de Paolo Giovio', ('Intercultural exchange and transfer of representations of Turkish portraits of Paolo Giovio'), Université de Genève,' Arborescences: revue d'études françaises, n° 2, 2012, pp.6-7, accessed August 23, 2014, http://www.erudit.org/apropos/utilisation.html
98. Jörn Rüsen, "What is Historical Consciousness? - A Theoretical Approach to Empirical Evidence," trans. Wolfgang Gebhard. Paper presented at Canadian Historical Consciousness in an International Context: Theoretical Frameworks, University of British Columbia, Vancouver, BC, 2001, 4.
99. D. Soyini Madison, *Critical Ethnography: Method, Ethics, and Performance* (Los Angeles: Sage Publications, 2012), 58.
100. Madison, *Critical Ethnography*, 58.
101. Sa'i, *Sinan's Autobiographies*, 130.

102. '…bu şerh ü tafsili sahayıf-ı rüzgârda nümüne ü yādgār kalmak içün.' See Sa'i, *Sinan's Autobiographies*, 62, 59.
103. 'her küngüre-'i eyvāndan bir gūşe ve her zāviye-'i virāndan bir tūşe peydā eyleyūp ... ' See Sa'i, Sinan's Autobiographies, 115, 142.
104. Sa'i, *Sinan's Autobiographies*, 74, 85, 156.
105. Sa'i, *Sinan's Autobiographies*, 65, 75, 85. For definitions of Ottoman-Turkish words see Yeni Cep Lügat.
106. 'günden güne envā'-i 'imaretler ihtira' olınup nezāket izdiyād bulmışdur ...'. See Sa'i, *Sinan's Autobiographies*, 65, 78, 131.
107. Sa'i, *Sinan's Autobiographies*, 74-75.
108. Sa'i, *Sinan's Autobiographies*, 74.
109. Sa'i, *Sinan's Autobiographies*, 123.
110. See Giorgio Vasari, Preface to Part I, *The Lives*.
111. Sa'i, *Sinan's Autobiographies*, 123, 131.
112. Selen B. Morkoç, 'Reading Architecture from the text: The Ottoman Story of the Four Marble Columns,' accessed February 9, 2018. https://www.academia.edu/27608699/Reading_Architecture_from_Text_The_Story_of_the_Four_Marble_Columns, 34.
113. Sa'i, *Sinan's Autobiographies*, 122.
114. Lowenthal, *The Past is a Foreign Country* (Cambridge: Cambridge University Press, 1985), 339.
115. Gülru Necipoğlu-Kafadar, *Muqarnas*, Vol. 3 (1985): 92-117, BRILL, accessed 8 Feb, 2018http://www.jstor.org/stable/1523086?origin=JSTOR-pdf, 92.
116. Rüsen, 'What is Historical Consciousness?', 4.
117. Vasari, Preface to Part I, *The Lives*.
118. See Vasari, Part III of *The Lives*, http://members.efn.org/~acd/vite/VasariMichelangelo8.html; and Sa'i, *Sinan's Autobiographies*, 74-75.
119. 'Nicomachean Ethics of Aristotle,' Book IV, http://www.sacred-texts.com/cla/ari/nico/nico036.htm
120. 'Ayasōfya gibi qubbe aslā yapılmaz diyu bahs eyledi dünyā / Bu 'ālī qubbe andan oldı a'zam ... bir cami' binâsına emr-i hūmāyūnları oldı ki rüzgârda misāl olmaya.' See Sa'i, Sinan's Autobiographies, 130, 150.
121. Sa'i, *Sinan's Autobiographies*, 66.
122. Sa'i, *Sinan's Autobiographies*, 66.
123. Sinan makes references to 'tecdid' and 'zuhūrat' in his autobiographies describing his works, see pp. 71, 78, 79, 85; *Tecdid* literally means, restore, give rebirth, renovate, renew; *zuhur / zuhūrat* means, bring to life, to create anew, perfection. See Ottoman-Turkish Dictionary, *Yeni Cep Lügat*, 325, 327.
124. See *Yeni Cep Lügat*, 128. *Ihya*: diriltme, canlandırma, şenlendirme, (literal translation: rebirth, resurrect, renovate, restore).
125. See Mustafa Selaniki Efendi, *Tarih-i Selaniki*, edited by Mehmet Ipsirli, 2 vols (Istanbul: Türk Tarih Kurum Basımevi, 1989), I: 95-96.
126. 'Murādım caāmi-i şerifi ihyā idüb eşer-i haāşş idinmekdür.' See Mustafa Selaniki Efendi, *Tarih-i Selaniki*, 120-121.
127. See Vasari, Preface to Part I, *The Lives*, and Part III, http://members.efn.org/~acd/vite/VasariMichelangelo8.html
128. Başbakanlık Arşivi, Istanbul, Muhimme Defteri 22, no. 171, 82.
129. Also see Ahmed Refik, On Altıncı, no. 18 (1935): 22-24 and partial translation in 'Hagia Sophia and the First Minaret Erected After the Conquest of Constantinople,'

by William Emerson and Robert L. Van Nice, in *American Journal of Archaeology*, Vol. 54, No. 1 (Jan. - Mar., 1950): 33-34.

130. Atıl, *Süleymanname*, 206.
131. Oleg Grabar, *The Formation of Islamic Art* (New Haven and London: Yale University Press, 1987), 49, 51, 63, 68.
132. Grabar, *The Formation of Islamic Art*, 49, 51, 63, 68.
133. Grabar, *The Formation of Islamic Art*, 49, 51, 63, 68.
134. Sa'i, *Sinan's Autobiographies*, 66, 79.
135. Başbakanlık Arşivi, Muhimme Defteri 10, no. 391, 253, dated 19B, 979, Istanbul.
136. A c.1581 miniature painting by Lokman depicts Ottoman architects and craftsmen working at the Holy Precinct.
137. Gülru Necipoğlu, *The Age of Sinan: Architectural Culture in the Ottoman Empire* (London: Reaktion Books, 2005), 168.
138. Vasari, Preface to Part II, *The Lives*, http://members.efn.org/~acd/vite/VasariPreface2.html
139. Sa'i, *Sinan's Autobiographies*, 150.

2. THE MEDITERRANEAN RENAISSANCE: A SHARED HERITAGE

1. Claire Norton, "Blurring the Boundaries: Intellectual and Cultural Interactions between Eastern and Western: Christian and Muslim Worlds," in *The Renaissance and the Ottoman World*, ed. Anna Contadini and Claire Norton (England: Ashgate Publishing Limited, 2013), 4.
2. See Raphaela Lewis, *Everyday Life on Ottoman Turkey* (UK: Dorset, 1988), 131; and Andre Clot, *Suleiman the Magnificent* (London: Saqi, 2005).
3. See C. Kafadar, *Between Two Worlds: The Construction of the Ottoman State* (Berkeley: University of California Press, 1995), xi; also see John M. Najemy, *Italy in the Age of the Renaissance 1300-1550* (New York: Oxford University Press, 2004).
4. For Ottoman Renaissance during the reign of Mehmed II see Julian Raby, "A Sultan of Paradox: Mehmed the Conqueror as a patron of the art," *Oxford Art Journal*, Vol. 5, No. 1, Patronage (1982): 3-8, Oxford University Press, accessed May 15, 2015, http://www.jstor.org/stable/1360098. Also see Franz Babinger, *Mehmed the Conqueror and His Time*, trans. R. Manheim (Princeton: Princeton University Press, 1978); E. Stamoulos, *Mehmed II's Portraits: Patronage, Historiography and the Early Modern Context* (Montreal: McGill University, 2005); also for the period during the reign of Süleyman the Magnificent see Halil Inalcık, *The Ottoman Empire - The Classical Age 1300-1600* (London: Phoenix, 1994); Norman Itzkowitz, *Ottoman Empire and Islamic Tradition* (Chicago: University of Chicago Press, 1980); Metin Mustafa, *The Ottoman Renaissance: A Reconsideration of Early Modern Ottoman Art, 1413-1575* (New Jersey: Blue Dome Press 2019); Lord Kinross, *The Ottoman Centuries - The Rise and Fall of the Turkish Empire* (U.S: Quill, 1990); Bernard Lewis, *Cultures In Conflict - Christian, Muslim, and Jews in the Age of Discovery* (New York: Oxford University Press, 1995); Karen Barkey, *Empire of Difference: The Ottomans in Comparative Perspective* (United Kingdom: Cambridge University Press, 2008); Kemal Karpat & Yetkin Yıldırım, *The Ottoman Mosaic: Preservation of minority groups, Religious tolerance, Governance of Ethnically diverse societies* (Seattle: Cune Press, 2010); Ebru Boyar and Kate Fleet, *A Social History of Ottoman Istanbul* (United Kingdom: Cambridge Univer-

sity Press, 2010); Gülru Necipoğlu and Alina Payne, eds., *Histories of Ornament: From Global to Local* (Princeton: Princeton University Press, 2016).

5. Nancy Bisaha, *Creating East West: Renaissance Humanists and the Ottoman Turks* (Philadelphia: University of Pennsylvania Press, 2006), 174.
6. Ibid., 174.
7. Friedrich Adler, 'Die Moscheen zu Constantinopel: Eine architektonische baugeschictliche Studie,' (The Mosques of Constantinople: An Architectural Study), *Deutsche Bauzeitung* 8 (1874): 65–66, 73–76, 81–83, 89–91, 97– 99.
8. See Corneilus Gurlitt, *Istanbul'un Mimari Sanatı, Architecture of Constantinople, Die Baukunst Konstantinopels* translated by Rezan Kæzæltan (Ankara: Enformasyon ve Dokumantasyon Hizmetleri Vakfı, 1999), 59, 66, 96. The work has been translated from Cornelius Gurlitt, *Die Baukunst Konstantinopels*, 2 vols. (Berlin: 1907).
9. Gurlitt, *Istanbul'un Mimari Sanatı.*
10. See Franz Babinger, 'Die türkische Renaissance: Bemerkungen zum Schaffen des grossen türkischen Baumeisters Sinân,' *Beiträge zur Kenntnis des Orients* 9 (1914): 67–88.
11. Franz Babinger, 'Ein osmanischer Michelangelo,' *Frankfurter Zeitung*, Sept. 7, 1915, no. 248.
12. Ernst Diez, *Türk Sanatı: Başlangıcından Günümüze Kadar*, trans. Oktay Aslanapa, (Istanbul, 1946), 232.
13. Diez, *Türk Sanatı*, 232.
14. Diez, *Türk Sanatı*, 6–7, 27, 138–39, 170, 192–98. Also see Halil Inalcık, *The Ottoman Empire: The Classical Age 1300–1600*, (London: Butler & Tanner, 1973).
15. Esin Atıl, *Süleymanname: The Illustrated History of Süleyman the Magnificent* (Washington: National Gallery of Art, 1986), 31. Also see *The Age of Süleyman the Magnificent*, (NSW, Australia: Art Exhibitions Australia / Beagle Press, 1990, Exhibition Publication); also see Esin Atıl, 'The Image of Süleyman in Ottoman Art,' in *Süleyman the Second and His Time*, edited by Halil Inalcik and Cemal Kafadar (Istanbul: The Isis Press, 2010), 333–341.
16. For more on this see the Essays V, VI, XI and XII in this book.
17. For more on this see the essay "VII. The Iconography of Renaissance Ceremonials in the Early Modern World" in this book.
18. Edward Said, *Orientalism* (London: Penguin Books, 1995), 342-343.
19. Z. Sardar, *Orientalism* (Buckingham: Open University Press, 1999), vii.
20. Ibid., 31.
21. Norton, "Blurring the Boundaries: Intellectual and Cultural Interactions between Eastern and Western: Christian and Muslim Worlds", 3.
22. See Homi Bhabha, *The Location of Cultures* (London & New York: Routledge, 1994), Kindle edition.
23. See David Abulafia, *The Great Sea: A Human History of the Mediterranean* (New York: Oxford University Press, 2011).
24. Norton, "Blurring the Boundaries: Intellectual and Cultural Interactions between Eastern and Western: Christian and Muslim Worlds", 4.
25. See Fernand Braudel, *The Mediterranean and the Mediterranean World in the Age of Philip II*, Vols. 1 and II, (London: Fontana Press, 1972).
26. For more see Inalcık, *The Ottoman Empire: The Classical Age 1300-1600.*
27. Braudel, *The Mediterranean*, Vol. 1, 543-544.
28. Ibid., 550.
29. Paul Coles, *The Ottoman Impact on Europe* (London: Thames and Hudson, 1968), back cover.

30. Ibid.
31. Lisa Jardine and Jerry Brotton, *Global Interest: Renaissance Art Between East and West* (London: Reaktion Books, 2000), 61.
32. Ibid., 61.
33. Ibid., 61.
34. Ibid., 61.
35. Ibid., 61.
36. Gerald MacClean, "Introduction: Re-Orienting the Renaissance", in *Re-Orienting the Renaissance*, ed. Gerald MacClean (New York: Palgrave Macmillan, 2005), 8.
37. Lisa Jardine, *Worldly Goods: A New History of the Renaissance* (London: W. W. Norton & Company, 1996), back cover.
38. See Deborah Howard, *Venice and the East, The Impact of the Islamic World in Venetian Architecture 1100-1500* (New Haven and London: Yale University Press, 2000).
39. Ibid., 218.
40. Rosamond E. Mack, *Bazaar to Piazza: Islamic Trade and Italian Art, 1300-1600* (California: University of California, 2002), 179.
41. J. Goody, *Renaissances: The One or the Many?* (New York: Cambridge University Press, 2010), 7.
42. Ibid., 7.
43. Ibid., 4.
44. Ibid., 1-6.
45. Ibid., 138.
46. Ibid., 138.
47. See Najemy, *Italy in the Age of the Renaissance 1300-1550*. Also see Mustafa, *The Ottoman Renaissance*.
48. See Metin Mustafa, *The Ottoman Renaissance: A Reconsideration of Early Modern Ottoman Art 1413-1575* (New Jersey: Blue Dome Press, 2019); also see Gülru Necipoğlu, *The Age of Sinan: Architectural Culture in the Ottoman Empire* (London: Reaktion Books, 2005).
49. See Abulafia, *The Great Sea*.
50. Ibid.
51. Ibid.
52. See Babinger, *Mehmed the Conqueror and His Time*.
53. William Dalrymple, "Foreword: The Process of Frontiers of Islam and Christendom: A Clash or Fusion of Civilisations?" in *Re-Orienting the Renaissance: Cultural Exchanges with the East*, ed. G. MacLean (New York: Palgrave, 2005), xv.
54. See Giancarlo Casale, *The Ottoman Age of Exploration* (Oxford, New York: Oxford University Press, 2010).
55. Dalrymple, "Foreword: The Process of Frontiers of Islam and Christendom," xv.
56. Goody, *Renaissances: The One or the Many?* 19.
57. Robert Ousterhout, "The East, the West, and the Appropriation of the Past in Early Ottoman Architecture", Vol, 43, no. 2 (2004): 165, *International Center of Medieval Art*, accessed March 24, 2015, http://www.jstor.org/stable/25067103.
58. See H. G. Yurdaydın, *Matrakçi Nasuh* (Ankara: Türk Tarih Kurumu, 1963); E. Atıl, "Art and Architecture", in *History of the Ottoman State, Society and Civilization*, II (Istanbul: IRCICA, 2002), 617-618.
59. N. Avcıoğlu, "Istanbul: The Palimpsest City in Search of Its Architext," in *Anthropology and Aesthetics* 53-54 (Spring-Autumn, 2008): 194, accessed March 25, 2015, http://www.jstor.org/stable/25608817194
60. Ibid., 193.

61. P. Mansel, *Constantinople: City of the World's Desire, 1453-1924* (London: John Murray, 1996), 27.
62. E. Muir, "Representations of Power", in *Italy in the Age of Renaissance*, ed. John M. Najemy New York: Oxford University Press, 2009), 239; also see E. Muir, "Images of Power: Art and Pageantry in Renaissance Venice," *American Historical Review* 84 (1979): 16-52.
63. Ibid., 239.
64. Ibid., 240. For more see Metin Mustafa, "Iconography of Renaissance ceremonials in the Early Modern World," *Australian Journal of Islamic Studies* 3, 1 (2018): 1-23.
65. Mansel, *Constantinople*, 42.
66. For more on Renaissance city see, 'Essay III - The Iconography of Renaissance Ceremonials in the Early Modern World' in this book.
67. Leon Batista Alberti, *On the Art of Building in Ten Books*, ed. Joseph Rykwert, Neil Leach and Robert Tavenor (Cambridge MA and London: MIT Press, 1989), 195-199.
68. Spiro Kostof, *A History of Architecture: Settings and Rituals*, New York, Oxford, 1985, p.459.
69. Esin Atıl, *Süleymanname: The Illustrated History of Süleyman the Magnificent* (Washington: National Gallery of Art, 1986), 31. Also see *The Age of Süleyman the Magnificent* (New South Wales, Australia: Art Exhibitions Australia / Beagle Press, 1990, Exhibition Publication).
70. Ibid., 31.
71. Esin Atıl, "Ottoman Miniature Painting under Sultan Mehmed II", *Ars Orientalis* Vol: 9 (1973): 103-120.
72. Ibid., 119-120.
73. Ibid., 103-120.
74. For more on the portrait of Mehmed II by Costanzo de Ferraro 's pupil Ahmed of Bursa see Gülru Necipoğlu, 'From Byzantine Constantinople to Ottoman Konstantiniyye: Creation of a Cosmopolitan Capital and Visual Culture Under Sultan Mehmed II,' in *From Byzantium to Istanbul: 8000 Years of Capital*, ed. Nazan Ölçer (Istanbul: Sabanci University, Sakip Sabanci Museum, 2010), 265-276. Sixteenth century Ottoman scholar Mustafa Ali, however, in his *Epic Deeds of Artists* claims that Ahmed was Sinan Bey's pupil. See Mustafa Ali, *Epic Deeds of Artists*, edited, translated and commented by Esra Akin-Kivanc (Leiden: Brill, 2011), 286.
75. Claire Norton, "Blurring the Boundaries: Intellectual and Cultural Interactions between Eastern and Western: Christian and Muslim Worlds," in *The Renaissance and the Ottoman World*, ed. Anna Contadini and Claire Norton (England: Ashgate Publishing Limited, 2013), 11.
76. Ayşe Çötellioğlu, *Topkapı Palace Museum collection of paintings and Portraits of the Sultans* (Istanbul: Bilkent Kültür Girişimi Publications, 2012), 30. For the connection between Paolo Giovio and Nakkaş Osman also see Nurhan Atasoy, "Nakkaş Osman'ın Padişah Portreleri Albümü," *Turkiyemiz* 6 (1972): 2-12.
77. J. Brotton, *The Renaissance: A Very Short Introduction* (New York: Oxford University Press, 2006, 8.
78. Selda Besnier-Kılıçoğlu, "Sinan and Palladio: The Parallel development of two master-builders," accessed June 14, 2015, http://unesdoc.unesco.org/images/0007/000781/078126eo.pdf#77905, 34.
79. Ibid., 34.
80. R. Wittkower, *Architectural Principles in the Age of Humanism* (New York: W. W. Norton & Company Inc., 1972), 57-76.

81. S. Yerasimos, *Constantinople: Istanbul's Historical Heritage* (Paris: H. F. Ullmann Publishing, 2012), 276. Also see Henry Matthews, "Rethinking Ottoman Architecture," paper presented at the ACSA International Conference, 2001; Brian Sewell, "Sinan: The Architect of a Forgotten Renaissance," *Cornucopia*, 1992/93.
82. Besnier-Kılıçoğlu, "Sinan and Palladio," 34.
83. See Ali, *Epic Deeds of Artists*, 121, 130, 135, 268.
84. Buthayna Eilouti, "Sinan and Palladio: Two Cultures and Nine Squares," *International Journal of Architectural Heritage: Conservation, Analysis, and Restoration* 6, 1 (2011): 12, accessed June 29, 2015, DOI: 10.1080/15583058.2010.495821.
85. Besnier-Kılıçoğlu, "Sinan and Palladio," 34.
86. See Selen B. Morkoç, "An Architect to Challenge Them All: Sinan Phenomenon in Architectural Historiography," *Fabrications: The Journal of the Society of Architectural Historians, Australia and New Zealand* 19, no. 1 (June 2009): 15; also see Ascanio Condivi, *The Life of Michelangelo*, trans., Alice Sedgwick Wohl (Oxford: Phaidon Press Limited, 1976); Antonio di Tuccio Manetti, *The Life of Brunelleschi*, trans., Catherine Engass (Pennsylvania: Pennsylvania State University Press, 1970).
87. Spiro Kostof, *A History of Architecture: Settings and Rituals* (2nd ed.), (Oxford: Oxford University Press, 1995), 461; also see Metin Mustafa, *Michelangelo meets Sinan: Representations of the Divine, Salvation and Paradise* (Sydney: Centre for Ottoman Renaissance and Civilisation, 2021).
88. See Kostof, *A History of Architecture*, 461; also see Godfrey Goodwin, *A History of Ottoman Architecture* (London: Thames & Hudson, 1971); Doğan Kuban, *Ottoman Architecture* (Suffolk: Antique Collectors Club Distributors, 2010).
89. Sa'i, *Sinan's Autobiographies*, 66, 74-75.
90. '...bu şerh ü tafsili sahayıf-ı rüzgârda nümüne ü yādgār kalmak içün.' See Sa'i, *Sinan's Autobiographies*, 62, 59.
91. Sa'i, Sinan's Autobiographies, 74, 85, 156.
92. Sa'i, *Sinan's Autobiographies*, 65, 75, 85. For definitions of Ottoman-Turkish words see Yeni Cep Lügat.
93. 'günden güne envā'-i 'imaretler ihtira' olınup nezāket izdiyād bulmışdur ...'. See Sa'i, *Sinan's Autobiographies*, 65, 78, 131.
94. Sa'i, *Sinan's Autobiographies*, 74-75.
95. Spiro Kostof, *A History of Architecture: Settings and Rituals* (New York: Oxford University Press, 1985), 459.
96. Necipoğlu, *The Age of Sinan*, 13-23.
97. Henry A. Milton and Craig Hugh Smyth, *Michelangelo Architect: The Façade of San Lorenzo and the Drum of the Dome of St. Peter's* (Milan: Olivetti, 1988), 102. Also see Joseph Connors, 'Borromini, Hagia Sophia, and S. Vitale', in *Architectural Studies in Memory of Richard Krautheimer*, ed. Cecil Striker (Mainz: Verlag Philipp Von Zabern, 1996), 43-48.
98. For the building of the Süleymaniye Mosque dates see Mustafa Sa'i, *Sinan's Autobiographies: Five Sixteenth Century Texts*, Introductory Notes, Critical Editions, and Translations by Howard Crane and Esra Akın, edited by Gülru Necipoğlu (Leiden: Brill, 2006).
99. For St. Peter's see F. Hartt, *History of Italian Renaissance Art* (6th ed.) (Englewood Cliffs: Prentice Hall, 2006).
100. See Connors, 'Borromini, Hagia Sophia, and S. Vitale', 43-48.
101. Ibid., 45.
102. For more on this, see Henry A. Milton and V. Lampugnani, eds. *The Renaissance from Brunelleschi to Michelangelo: The Representation of Architecture* (Milan: Rizzoli,

1994), 612, 645, 658-64.
103. See Jean-Claude Flachat, 1766, cited in Necipoğlu, *The Age of Sinan,* 102.
104. Francesco Dei Marchi, cited in Necipoğlu, *The Age of Sinan,* 101.
105. See Howard Burns, "Building and Construction in Palladio's Vicenza" in *Les Chantiers de la renaissance,* ed. A. Chastel and J. Guillaume (Paris: Piccard, 1991), 191-226.
106. See Morkoc, "An Architect to Challenge Them All," 15; also see Necipoğlu, *The Age of Sinan,* 13, 15.
107. Fontenelle cited in Goody, *Renaissances: The One or the Many?* 9. On Ottoman-Turkish humanism refer to Talat S. Halman, *Rapture and Revolution: Essays on Turkish Literature* (New York: Syracuse University Press, New York, 2007).
108. Mustafa Sa'i, *Sinan's Autobiographies: Five Sixteenth Century Texts,* Introductory Notes, Critical Editions, and Translations by Howard Crane and Esra Akın, ed. Gülru Necipoğlu (Leiden: Brill, 2006), 115, 142.
109. Alberti, Alberti, *On the Art of Building in Ten Books,* 24.
110. Sa'i, *Sinan's Autobiographies,* 12, 22, 58-59.
111. Qur'an cited in Sa'i, *Sinan's Autobiographies,* 59.
112. Ibid., 64-65.
113. Ibid., 122-133.
114. For more see Mustafa, *The Ottoman Renaissance.*
115. F. Borghesi, M. Papio and M. Riva eds., *Pico Della Mirandola: Oration on the Dignity of Man, A New Translation and Commentary* (New York: Cambridge University Press, 2012), 109.
116. M. Rogers, "The Arts Under Süleyman the Magnificent", in *Süleyman the Second and His Time,* eds. H. Inalcik and C. Kafadar (Istanbul: The Isis Press, 2010), 257.
117. Ibid., 263.
118. Ibid., 261.
119. Esin Atıl, *Turkish Art* (Washington and New York: Smithsonian Institution Press, 1980), 139.
120. Ibid., 231-232.
121. Atıl, "Ottoman Miniature Painting," 120.
122. Alexandrine N. St. Clair, "Turkengefahr," in *Islamic Art in the Metropolitan Museum,* ed. Richard Ettinghausen (New York: Metropolitan Museum of Art, 1972), 319.
123. Niccolo Machiavelli, "Discourses on Livy," in *The Prince and the Discourses,* trans. by Luigi Ricci (New York: Modern Library College, 1950), 182.
124. See James Bruce Ross and Mary M. McLaughlin, eds. *The Portable Renaissance Reader* (New York: Penguin Books, 1977).
125. Sheila Hale, *Titian: His Life* (UK: Harper Collins, 2012) UK, accessed August 11, 2015, http://books.google.com.au/books?id=rnwyXxHiGzUC&printsec=frontcover&dq=inauthor:%22Sheila+Hale%22&hl=en&sa=X&ei=TKM6Ubm1JsXKmgWytoCYDQ&ved=0CDcQ6AEwAQ#v=onepage&q&f=false
126. For more see Brotton, *The Renaissance.*
127. Filiz Yenişehirlioğlu, "Ottoman Ceramics in European Contexts", *Muqarnas,* Vol. 21 (2004): 373, accessed August 29, 2015, http://www.jstor.org/discover/10.2307/1523369?
128. Ibid., 379.
129. Ibid., 380.
130. Ibid., 373.

3. THE ICONOGRAPHY OF RENAISSANCE CEREMONIALS IN THE EARLY MODERN WORLD

1. See Giorgio Vasari, *Vasari's Lives of the Artists,* trans. Jonathan Foster (New York: Dover Publications, 2005), Kindle edition.
2. J. R. Mulryne, Maria Ines Aliverti and Anna Maria Testaverde, *Ceremonial Entries in Early Modern Europe: The Iconography of Power* (England: Ashgate, 2015), vii.
3. Matteo Burioni, *Vasari's Rinascita: History, Anthropology or Art Criticism* (Leiden, The Netherlands: Koninklijke Brill NV, 2010), accessed March 14, 2014, https://www.academia.edu/2638258/Vasari_s_rinascita._History_anthropology_or_art_criticism, 117.
4. Jerry Brotton, *The Renaissance: A Very Short Introduction* (New York: Oxford University Press, 2006), 8.
5. For more on the influence of Ottoman military music on Italian stage interludes, see T. D. Taylor, *Beyond Exoticism. Western Music and the World* (Durham and London: Duke University Press, 2007), 8, 20-21.
6. For a list of sixteenth-century printed costume books, see Joanne Olian, "Sixteenth Century Books," *Costume* 3 (1977): 20-48.
7. For more on imitating the 'Other', see Edward Said, *Orientalism* (London, UK: Penguin Books, 1995).
8. Niccolò Machiavelli, "Discourses on Livy," in *The Prince and the Discourses,* ed. and trans. Luigi Ricci (New York: Modern Library, 1950), 182.
9. Homi K. Bhabha, *The Location of Culture* (New York: Routledge, 2004), Kindle Edition.
10. Ibid.
11. Ibid.
12. Ibid.
13. Ibid.
14. Ibid.
15. Philip Mansel, *Constantinople: City of the World's Desire, 1453-1924* (London, UK: John Murray, 1995), 80.
16. N. Menemencioğlu ed., *The Penguin Verse of Turkish Verse* (Suffolk, UK: Penguin Books Ltd., 1978), 108.
17. Marquis de Nointel, cited in Mansel, *Constantinople,* 80.
18. Mansel, *Constantinople,* 80.
19. Mustafa Selaniki Efendi, *Tarih-i Selaniki,* vol. 1., ed. Mehmet Ispirli (Istanbul: Türk Tarih Kurum Basımevi, 1989), 131-136.
20. Derin Terzioğlu, "The Imperial Circumcision Festival of 1582: An Interpretation," *Muqarnas* 12 (1995): 97. Also see Stephane Yerasimos, "The Imperial Procession: Recreating a World's Order," in *Surname-i Vehbi,* accessed September 23, 2014, http://web.archive.org/web/20091025054327/http://geocities.com/surnamei_vehbi/yerasimos.html.
21. Gülru Necipoğlu, "Süleyman the Magnificent and Representations of Power in the Context of Ottoman-Habsburg Papal Rivalry," *The Art Bulletin* 71, no. 3 (1989), 401, accessed August 3, 2014, http://www.jstor.org/stable/3051136.
22. J. M. Saslow, *Florentine Festival as 'Theatrum Mundi': The Medici Wedding of 1589* (New Haven and London: Yale University Press, 1996), 2.
23. See George Young, *Constantinople* (New York: Dorset House Publishing Co Inc., 1997), 135.

24. Young, *Constantinople,*135. For more on the wedding ceremony see Leslie P. Peirce, *The Imperial Harem: Women and Sovereignty in the Ottoman Empire* (New York: Oxford University Press, 1993), 61-62.
25. See De'Ludovici's report to the Venetian senate delivered on June 3, 1534, in Eugenio Alberi, *Le Relazioni Dgli Ambasciatori Veneti,* serie 3, vol. 1:29 (Firenze: A Spese Dell'Editore, 1863), accessed June 14, 2015, https://archive.org/stream/E.AlberiRelazioniDegliAmbasciatoriVeneti-Serie3-Vol.1/Alberi.Vol.I_djvu.txt.
26. P. Tinagli, *Women in Italian Renaissance Art: Gender, Representation and Identity* (New York: Manchester University Press, 1997), 28.
27. Ibid.
28. Vasari, *Lives,* 170.
29. Letter of the *notaio* Bernardo Gamberelli to Cosimo de'Medici I, 29 March 1539, cited in *La Corte, il Mare, i Mercanti* (Firenze: Electa, 1980), filza 337, cc.134 e 137.
30. Anna Maria Testaverde, "The Book of Ceremonies of Francesco Tongiarini (1536-1612)," in *Ceremonial Entries in Early Modern Europe,* eds. J. R. Mulryne, Maria Ines Aliverti and Anna Maria Testaverde (Burlington, USA: Ashgate Publishing Company, 2015), 99.
31. For more, see Bhabha, *The Location of Culture.*
32. Discorso di Lodovico Alamanni sopra if fermare lo stato di Firenze nella Medici devozione de. Luigi Alamanni, cited in Testaverde "The Book of Ceremonies," 101.
33. L. L. Perkins, *Music in the Age of the Renaissance* (New York: W. W. Norton & Company, 1999), 395-396.
34. Mulryne, Aliverti and Testaverde, *Ceremonial Entries in Early Modern Europe,* 5.
35. Ibid., 5.
36. R. C. Trexler, *Public Life in Florence* (London: Cornell University Press, 1980), 475.
37. C. Pastore, "Bipolar Behavior: Ferdinando I de' Medici and the East," in *The Turk and Islam in the Western Eye, 1450-1750: Visual Imagery before Orientalism,* ed. J. G. Harper (New York: Taylor & Francis, 2011), 129. Also see Saslow, *Florentine Festival as 'Theatrum Mundi.'*
38. David Rosand, *Myths of Venice: The Figuration of a State* (Library of Congress, Washington DC: University of North Carolina Press, 2001), 1-2.
39. Charles Dempsey, cited in David Rosand, "Myths of Venice: The Figuration of a State," *Renaissance Quarterly* 56, no. 2 (2003): 454, accessed July 15, 2014, http://www.jstor.org/stable/1261857.
40. J. Paoletti and G. M. Radke, *Art in Renaissance Italy* (London: Laurence King Publishing, 2005), 490.
41. Ibid., 490.
42. Ibid., 490.
43. Ibid., 490.
44. Ibid., 490.
45. Rosand, *Myths of Venice,* 14.
46. Ibid., 13-14.
47. Ibid., 14.
48. Ibid., 14.
49. Halil Inalcık, *The Middle East and the Balkans under the Ottoman Empire* (Bloomington: Indiana University Turkish Studies Department, 1993), 28.
50. Muslims believe Abraham took Hagar and Ishmael to the Valley of Baca (mentioned in Psalms 84:6, "Who passing through the valley of Baca make it a well; the rain also filleth the pools"). Muslims believe the valley of Baca to be the ancient site of Mecca. After leaving Hagar and Ishmael, the boy was saved by the Zam Zam water that

sprung from beneath his feet. Although the Qur'an does not mention this, the hadiths of the Prophet elucidate this narrative in more detail. See hadiths of the Prophet by Bukhara in M. Muhsin Khan, trans., *The Translation of the Meanings of Summarized Sahih Al-Bukhari: Arabic-English* (Lahore: Kazi Publications Inc., 1995).

51. See Genesis 17:5.
52. H. Aydın, *Pavilion of the Sacred Relics: The Sacred Trusts, Topkapi Palace Museum* (Istanbul, Clifton, USA: Tughra Books, 2011), 80.
53. See hadiths of Prophet Muhammad by Ibn Katheer Dimashqi, *Book of the End: Great Trials and Tribulations*, trans. Faisal Shafiq (Riyadh: Darussalam, 2006), 75-77.
54. Colin Imber, *The Ottoman Empire, 1300-1650: The Structure of Power* (New York: Palgrave Macmillan, 2002), 106.
55. Loren Partridge and Randolf Starn, *Arts of Power: Three Halls of State in Italy, 1300-1600* (Berkeley and Los Angeles: University of California Press, 1992), 211.
56. Thierry Hentsch, *Imagining the Middle East* (Montreal: Black Rose Books, 1992), 139.

www.ingramcontent.com/pod-product-compliance
Lightning Source LLC
LaVergne TN
LVHW050649100826
845148LV00011B/2045

9780646835440